Mechanical Creations in 3D

A Practical Look into Complex and Technical Setups for Animation & VFX

Mechanical Creations in 3D

A Practical Look into Complex and Technical Setups for Animation & VFX

Stewart Jones

CRC Press
Taylor & Francis Group
Boca Raton London New York

CRC Press is an imprint of the
Taylor & Francis Group, an **informa** business

CRC Press
Taylor & Francis Group
6000 Broken Sound Parkway NW, Suite 300
Boca Raton, FL 33487-2742

© 2019 by Taylor & Francis Group, LLC
CRC Press is an imprint of Taylor & Francis Group, an Informa business

No claim to original U.S. Government works

Printed on acid-free paper

International Standard Book Number-13: 978-1-138-56049-9 (Paperback)
978-1-138-56050-5 (Hardback)

Library of Congress Cataloging-in-Publication Data

Names: Jones, Stewart, 1984- author.
Title: Mechanical creations in 3D : a practical look into complex and technical
setups for animation & VFX / Stewart Jones.
Description: Boca Raton, FL : CRC Press/Taylor & Francis Group, 2019. |
Includes bibliographical references and index.
Identifiers: LCCN 2018033438| ISBN 9781138560499 (pbk. : acid-free paper) |
ISBN 9781138560505 (hardback : acid-free paper)
Subjects: LCSH: Cinematography--Special effects--Data processing. |
Machinery--Computer simulation. | Computer drawing--Special effects. |
Computer animation. | Three-dimensional display systems.
Classification: LCC TR858 .J66 2019 | DDC 777/.7--dc23
LC record available at https://lccn.loc.gov/2018033438

Visit the Taylor & Francis Web site at
http://www.taylorandfrancis.com

and the CRC Press Web site at
http://www.crcpress.com

Contents

Preface

"Rigging," "rigs," "riggers," "Technical Director (TD)," "Technical Animator"—when it comes to three dimensions (3D), two dimensions (2D), or computer graphics (CG) in general, these words, and the term "rigging," are often explicitly associated with characters or creatures—usually the heroes or villains, the protagonists or antagonists. Those are the kinds of rigs and rigging that get the most attention, at least. But, what about all of those other rigs? The unsung heroes of rigging? I'm talking about things that go unseen and unnoticed to the untrained eye, and even sometimes to the trained eye: digital doubles, secondary characters, creatures, crowds, animals, buildings, planes, trains, automobiles, cranes, props, and whatever else in 3D make-believe that needs articulation. Well, they are often forgotten by the audience and viewer, but without them, these fantastical visions that have been created for the screen would be missing something.

This book focuses on these kinds of "forgotten rigs." By creating a steampunk train that could easily be the main focal point for audiences, we take these rigs that are often found in the shadows and bring them into the light! Each element that we create for this steampunk locomotive can be used in a number of other situations, and for a variety of very different mechanical rigs. There are even uses for these kinds of setups in organic rigs too—you just need to get creative.

Throughout the creation of the steampunk locomotive rig, we'll combine both automated and manual rigging methodologies, while using techniques from hard-surface and organic rigging. Additionally, we will focus directly on systems that can be used for film and television—pretty much anything that is prerendered. However, with some tweaking here and there, the techniques and methods used in our approach to rigging this train could easily be adapted for real-time game engines if you need that. However, as that is not a focus for this book, you will need to understand not only the limitations of real-time rigs, but also of the nuances of whatever pipeline that you are using.

Mechanical Creations in 3D: A Practical Look into Complex and Technical Setups for Animation & VFX has been written for those needing a better understanding of complicated and technically challenging 3D setups. The text focuses on broken-down components with which the practices can be transplanted into other rigs. I hope that it will serve you as a guide to new or different strategies, and then be there as a reference guide for the rigs you create in the future.

Thank you for joining me on this journey. It's time to step onto that platform and get ready for the steampunk train to arrive at the station!

Acknowledgments

There are a number of people I owe a great deal to in both the creation and publication of this book, as well as many people who continuously and relentlessly help drive me forward. A few of these people are listed here:

- To Marie. I love you. You're amazing. Your contributions to my life, my work, and my soul are incalculable. You mean everything to me. I live for you. I live because of you. I'm forever thankful to you, and without you, I would be lost.
- My parents, my friends, Carol and Keith. Thank you for your continuous love and support. All of this is possible because of both of you, and the help, trust, and confidence that you always put into me. Thank you for being proud of me, and I hope you know how proud I am of both of you.
- Chris Rocks, buddy, as always, you came through for me and created an incredible asset to work with throughout this book. I really couldn't do this without you, so my deepest thanks for all that you have done. This time was really above and beyond… but more than that, thank you for being a friend and sharing the laughs along these journeys we seem to keep having. I promise—nothing this crazy ever again!
- We don't speak often, but Tina O'Hailey, thank you so much for always being approachable and kind. I don't think that this book would exist without your recommendation. One day, we need to grab a coffee together.
- Dave Bevans, thank you for sending me in the right direction, I appreciate it a lot. I hope that I get to work with you again.
- My editors, Sean Connely and Jessica Vega. Thank you both so much for the hard work, and for making this book a possibility. I sincerely appreciate your understanding with everything.

- Everyone who has helped me, either personally or professionally, thank you.

Finally, thank you to you! Yeah, you. The person reading this right now. Thank you very much for grabbing hold of this book and jumping into a complicated and challenging rig. There's lots to cover and loads to discover. Good luck on your journey.

Author

Stewart Jones is a writer, screenwriter, producer, and director, with experience in feature film, television, commercials, video games, and augmented and virtual reality. As an accomplished creative professional, his background includes both animation, live action, and visual effects (VFX) productions for worldwide clients. He is a full member of the Writers' Guild of Great Britain (WGGB), a published author, and a journal-published MBA graduate.

Currently, Stewart works as an independent freelancer providing writing, screenwriting, producing, and directing services for international clients and productions. Additionally, he holds training workshops throughout the year and can often be found speaking or teaching online and at various international conferences, colleges, and events. His previous roles include everything from animator to technical director (TD), and computer graphics (CG) supervisor or head of 3D to production manager.

For more information on Stewart, please check out the following links:

Personal Website: www.creatureattic.com
Twitter: twitter.com/creatureattic
LinkedIn: linkedin.com/in/stewart-jones/
Amazon Author: amazon.com/Stewart-Jones/e/B0091IL2U4
IMDb: imdb.me/stewartjones
WGGB: writersguild.org.uk/profile/?profile=2992

Contributor

As I have already mentioned in the "Acknowledgments" section, I really couldn't have created such an incredible steampunk train without the hard work and dedication of my good friend Chris Rocks. I've worked with Chris for a number of years on many different projects, and I'm proud to say that he is my go-to 3D artist for anything and everything.

I've been lucky enough to have Chris's assistance in the following three publications:

- Jones, S. (2012). *Digital Creature Rigging: The Art and Science of CG Creature Setup in 3ds Max.* USA, Focal Press.
- Jones, S. (2019). *Digital Creature Rigging: Wings, Tails and Tentacles.* USA, CRC Press.
- Jones, S. (2019). *Mechanical Creations in 3D: A Practical Look into Complex and Technical Setups for Animation & VFX.* USA, CRC Press.

Chris is available for freelance work, and I highly recommend him for any 3D production. Really, this guy is just the best! But, don't take my word for it—here is a short profile so you get a better understanding about him:

Chris has more than 20 years of digital experience in video games, TVC, marketing, advertising, education, medical, design, and VR/AR. In that time, he has worked on multiple award-winning productions including being an integral part of two BAFTA-winning projects. As a digital creative, his varied background has included working with UK and globally renowned brands in a multitude of roles.

Currently, Chris is a contract 3D visualizer working for an international technology company specializing in product development. His previous roles have included everything from 3D artist to creative director (CD), and computer graphics (CG) supervisor or art production manager.

For more information on Chris, please check out the following links:

Personal Website: www.tartanpimpernel.com
LinkedIn: linkedin.com/in/tartanpimpernel/

1

Introduction

All aboard!

Mind the gap as you step onto the train. Be careful of the closing doors … Yeah, I ran out of stereotypical train quotes pretty quickly. Anyway, welcome to the start of our steampunk-style train-rigging journey.

Throughout the next 10 chapters, we're going to be discussing theories, tips, tricks, and techniques for the three-dimensional (3D) rigging setup of complex, technical, hard-surface geometries. We're going to spend time looking into human-made, industrial-type machinery such as chains, tracks, cogs, dials, wires, and pistons, among others. Our goal is to design and create a system of hierarchies and controls that enables automation and overrides that an animator can control easily.

Although our primary creation is going to be a futuristic, steampunk-style train, the methodologies used here can be applied to a number of other hard objects. Cars, boats, planes, tanks, robots, and other kinds of vehicles or structures often need the same or similar kinds of rigs that we will be creating. And, as the way that we work on our rig throughout this book is modular, those rigged elements can be easily re-created and transplanted into other models and geometries. It is worth noting that, as with any rigging solution, there is no perfect way to create a rig. There are different options and choices to make, but we can create the best solution for the challenge at hand—which is what we do during the course of this book.

Our weapon of choice for this steampunk creation is Autodesk 3ds Max (3ds Max for short). At the time of writing, I'm using the latest version of the software, which is Autodesk 3ds Max 2019, but the approaches used in the rig's creation are transferrable to any of the more recent versions from around 2010 onward. I'm just guessing on this, but the fundamentals of 3ds Max haven't changed all that much over the years, so I'm pretty confident that things will work out just the same on older versions. Actually, even though I'm writing specifically about this software, the manner in which the rig is created can be shifted to other 3D software applications. Obviously, the tools and steps may be different, but the core foundations, techniques, and mathematics in which to create a rig are always the same…Honest! I have personally used both Autodesk 3ds Max and Autodesk Maya at a comparable level in professional productions, and although they have their differences (and quirks) in terms of architecture and procedures, both can replicate the exact same kinds of rigs. A good rig is a good rig and a bad rig is a bad rig in any program—so what I'm saying is that we better build a good one, no matter which software we're using!

One last thing: This book is aimed at those with an advanced level of understanding of 3D and a thorough knowledge of rigging tools and terminology. You also should be at least an intermediate-level user of 3ds Max, who can use the software confidently and comfortably. If you're new to rigging, I'm afraid to say that this book may, at times, be a little overwhelming. That's not to say that you won't be able to follow along—far from it, in fact. You definitely will be able to re-create the tutorials and enjoy creating most sections of the rig for the steampunk train, it's just that some of the foundations and core techniques of rigging aren't covered here, and you're really missing out if you don't understand everything that's going on.

All right! Welcome to *Mechanical Creations in 3D*. Let's take a practical look into complex and technical setups for animation and visual effects (VFX).

1.1 Chapter Overview

As I mentioned before, this book contains a total of 10 chapters. Within each chapter, we discuss, examine, and create various elements related to complex technical rigging setups. Specifically, we focus on practical exercises to create the rig elements, but we also cover some concepts and theoretical approaches as we go.

Let's take a moment to familiarize ourselves with what's coming up:

- *Chapter 1: Introduction*
  - This is where we are right now! In this chapter, we check out what we'll actually be doing in this book, we look at how this book is structured and how we can best use these structures, and we go through some

basic preparations and guidelines before jumping into the rigging of the steampunk locomotive.

- *Chapter 2: Model*
  - In this chapter, we step into the world of 3D for the first time. We discuss gathering references, how the concept of the steampunk train arrived, and we look at the geometry of the train using the 3 Stage Asset Build (3SAB) technique.
- *Chapter 3: Rigging Preparations*
  - During this chapter, we do some preparations that will help us to minimize possible complications as we move into the rigging process. These rigging preparations are relatively simple to do and provide us with cleaner scenes that are less likely to crash or become an unusable corrupt file.
- *Chapter 4: Common Rigging Techniques*
  - We then have a chapter dedicated to common rigging techniques that are used in 3ds Max for creating all kinds of rigs. This discussion serves as both an introduction to some of the tools that we need and as a refresher to those tools built into the software but not necessarily used very often. This is a great chapter that gives us the starting foundations for our rigging journey.
- *Chapter 5: Base Rig*
  - Here is where we start the main event—the first rigging stage of 3SAB. This chapter forms the foundation on which the more complex animation and automation rig will be built.
- *Chapter 6: Animation and Automation Rig—Part 1*
  - Probably the most complex chapter in this book, the animation and automation rig includes everything from basic and advanced tools to mathematical concepts like trigonometry and hypotenuse. In this chapter, we focus only on the first carriage. You see, the thing is, this phase of the rigging process is so big that it needs two chapters...
- *Chapter 7: Animation and Automation Rig—Part 2*
  - The second chapter in the Animation and Automation rigging process focuses on the second, third, and fourth carriages of the steampunk train. It is during this chapter where we set up the steampunk locomotive and all its technical features, making sure that they all work together correctly.
- *Chapter 8: Deformation Rig*
  - Although the final phase of the 3SAB, the deformation rig is often missing from mechanical setups because they do not need any further deformations. However, this does not mean that we can skip things. Rather, it just gives us another opportunity to enhance the functions and features of our rig, as well as a chance to look at some other techniques that we may have missed along the way.

- *Chapter 9: More Mechanical Rigging*
  - With the steampunk locomotive rig complete, we spend some time looking at additional mechanical rigging setups. These setups could be applied to the train rig that we have created, or they could just be helpful pointers for setups for any other mechanical rigs that you may be working on, now or in the future.
- *Chapter 10: Conclusion*
  - The final chapter summarizes the learning, rigging, testing, challenges, and creations that we have made throughout this entire book. We take a quick look over all the rigs that were created and discuss their uses. Then we wrap things up by thinking about what to do next and the journey ahead of us, which is far beyond the pages of this book.

1.2 Preparation

OK—now that we know what this book is all about and how it's structured, the next thing that we have to do is to make some preparations before we move forward. After all, failure to prepare is preparing to fail—or something like that.

The first thing I suggest is to grab hold of a pen and paper, or a notebook. This book aims to be a guide that you can refer to when needed, but I've always found that keeping my own notes helps me remember better. This is optional, of course, but it's always helped me, and I continue to add to my notebooks every day. No doubt you'll know about my love for notebooks if you've read any of my other published works, so I won't keep going on about it here!

Second, and I know this won't surprise you by any means, but, you're going to need a computer. It's unfortunate, but if you're following along with the intention of using Autodesk 3ds Max, you will be compelled to use a Microsoft Windows-based computer system. This is due to the programming architecture of 3ds Max being dependent upon Windows; it simply doesn't work without it. This limits our options of using alternatives such as Apple Mac or Linux. However, if you're planning on using another 3D application such as Autodesk Maya, Maxon Cinema 4D, or the open-source Blender, your options for computer hardware expand dramatically. This brings us to our next preparation step...

We also need some kind of 3D application—I know, big surprise! As previously stated, throughout this book, I am personally using Autodesk 3ds Max 2019, which is the latest available version to date. All guides and jargon found in this book are associated with this program, but if you're already skilled and practiced with rigging and/or other software, then you should be able to transfer the guides and techniques covered here to your preferred 3D software. After all, the principles and methods are common and relatively universal. If you'd like to follow along using Autodesk 3ds Max but you don't have access to the software, then you need to go and get it. The easiest way to do this is head on over to the Autodesk website (www.autodesk.com).

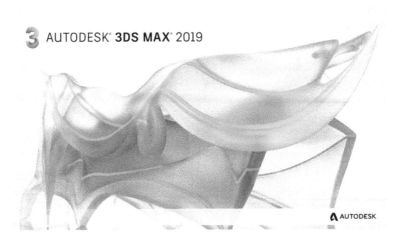

AUTODESK 3DS MAX 2019

A AUTODESK

Figure 1.1

Autodesk 3ds Max 2019 splash screen.

Browse through to the 3ds Max section, and along with information, demos, and specifications, you will be able to download the software. It's worth noting that Autodesk 3ds Max isn't available for free. In fact, it's a healthy chunk of change if you would like to purchase a license for commercial use. Luckily, there is a 30-day free trial, which should give you enough time to work through some of this book as well as assessing if 3ds Max is for you. There are also student and educator versions available. These are available for free, but you need to hit certain criteria in order to be granted one of these licenses, but it's definitely worth checking out (Figure 1.1).

Hmmm…What else?! Oh yeah, you're going to need some free time. It takes a while to work through all of this—I know because I've already been through it all! Now I'm no physician, but I also recommend snacks and beverages, plenty of sleep, some exercise, and some relaxing away from the computer and your 3D application of choice.

1.3 Art and Science

Rigging, like many aspects of 3D, requires the use of both hemispheres of the brain. We have to mix both art and science in order to create visually appealing rigs that are technically robust enough to endure the punishment that animation and the rest of the pipeline will throw at it (Figure 1.2).

Often, this is a daunting and challenging task. Making something look visually appealing and work great (art) requires a deep and methodical understanding of techniques, processes, and limitations of the software that we use (science). We have to keep in mind that the complicated technical setups (science) that we create needs to be intuitive and easy to use (art). Additionally, we have to create visually

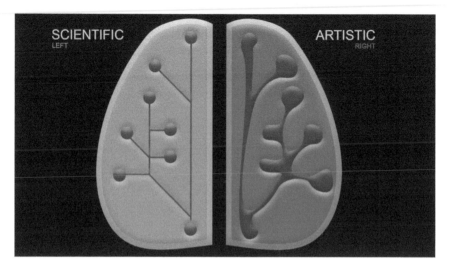

SCIENTIFIC
LEFT

ARTISTIC
RIGHT

Figure 1.2

Rigging and the creation of rigs requires a real mixture of the left and right sides of our brains, as illustrated here.

accurate rigs and deformations (art) that are driven by custom-built settings, setups, and mathematics (science). That's a lot of art and science going on.

1.4 Principles

Animators use 12 principles, aptly called "the 12 principles of animation." These principles, introduced in 1981, by Disney animators Ollie Johnston and Frank Thomas in their book,* have become the basis for animators and animation worldwide.

If you don't know these animation principles, I recommend that you familiarize yourself with them. After all, we're making rigs, rigs are used by animators, and animators use those principles, so it kind of makes sense that we know about them too.

These principles of animation are as follows:

1. Squash and Stretch
2. Anticipation
3. Staging
4. Straight Ahead and Pose to Pose
5. Follow Through and Overlapping Action
6. Slow In and Slow Out
7. Arcs

---

* *The Illusion of Life: Disney Animation*, New York, Abbeville Press.

8. Secondary Action
9. Timing
10. Exaggeration
11. Solid Drawing
12. Appeal

The thing is, for rigging in 3D, there are no widely adopted principles. Sure, there are some things that all rigs must do, how they perform, and how they behave, but there is nothing as solid as the 12 principles of animation for us to refer to quickly and easily. In another of my books,* I attempted to create a set of 12 rigging principles that could be used for creating any kind of rigs in 3D.

These are as follows:

1. *KISS!—Keep It Simple, Stupid!*: Rigs can be inherently complex. We create and link complicated setups, hierarchies, objects, codes, nodes, and many other things that are often confusing to others, and even ourselves at times! The aim with any 3D rigging is to keep that complexity away from others. To cover the confusing setups, we create an easy-to-use interface that is visually appealing and simple in comparison to what's really happening in the scene. There's a certain beauty in simplicity. Keep it simple, stupid!

2. *Planning*: Rushing into things without doing any planning is a sure-fire way to either set yourself up for failure or at least make things way more difficult than they have to be. It's better to be prepared for the worst than to hope for the best. So, remember to plan out your work before starting. Create some goals, make a checklist, have a schedule—whatever you think will help keep your plan on track.

3. *Research, Development, Resources*: Review your planning. Do you know how this rig is going to work? Is there a section that you're not sure about? Check over every aspect and highlight the more problematic setups that you're going to encounter. Research how you're going to create and rig those difficult sections. Develop solutions to those problems in isolation. Take those isolated setups and use them as an information resource or inspiration for when you jump into the full rig!

4. *Anatomy*: Anatomy is a branch of biology that studies the structures of living organisms. The study of anatomy is incredibly important for those of us who rig things in 3D. When it comes to organic models, it provides information on edge flows and topology, joint/bone placement, muscle systems, and flesh-deformation systems, among others. When it comes to hard-surface models like our train, this knowledge feeds into the wires, pivot points, and again, the topology of geometries.

5. *Biomechanics*: The topics of anatomy and biomechanics are closely related, but biomechanics focuses on the study of systems by the methods

---

* *Digital Creature Rigging: The Art and Science of CG Creature Setup in 3ds Max* (Jones, 2012).

of engineering mechanics. Putting this into practice for mechanical and hard-surface objects often requires some out-of-the-box thinking. For instance, the chain on a bike may have 40 links, and by regular thinking, that's 40 things to rig. However, if we incorporate a few of these principles, such as KISS and Biomechanics, we could conclude that although there are 40 links that all need to move, we simply need one Spline object and a Path Constraint (more on these later in this book) in order to simulate that we rigged each and every component.

6. *Flesh-Surface Deformation*: The term "flesh-surface deformation" refers to the deformation of geometry in 3D. Whether it's the initial binding/ skinning, muscle systems, blendshapes/morphs, cloth, hair, or fur, Flesh-Surface Deformation is the topic that covers all of this. Don't think that rigid surfaces aren't applicable here, because they are. At times, skinning is needed, and even blendshapes/morphs may be used to deform the solid structures.

7. *Animation*: You don't need to be an animator, but you do need an in-depth understanding of animation. You have to understand how your created rigs are going to be used, their limitations and quirks. The more knowledgeable you are about animation, the better you will be able to converse about rigs and animation.

8. *Modeling*: You don't have to be the greatest sculptor or modeler to create great rigs, but you do need the ability to edit geometry at a very high level. From directing edge flows and looping for deformation to creating face shapes or corrective shapes, it's an important principle to be able to use.

9. *Pipeline*: Having an understanding of the whole computer graphics (CG) pipeline, or at least the 3D pipeline, is important when rigging. If you're just creating things for yourself on a personal project, then you can work in the way that feels most comfortable. Of course, working with another person, or lots of people, requires more discipline and a greater understanding of what everyone else is doing and how your rigs affect their tasks and the broader pipeline.

10. *Dynamics*: Although we want to have as much control over our rigs as possible, there is a point at which having control over every tiny detail would be counterproductive. This can be where dynamics come into play. They allow us to automate certain movements that may not be practical or could be too time-consuming to animate manually. We can even allow dynamic rigs to be overwritten and manually animated on top of that, if it is really necessary. Dynamics can be used in anything from an exploding wall to a rope-bridge, or even in a character's tail—but no matter its use, it is an important principle for a rigger to know about.

11. *Scripting*: Scripting is another important principle for rigging. It allows us to automate the elements of a rig, automate the creation of rigs, and even

extend the 3D software that we're using. You can create your own tools, interfaces, and functions—and this opens up a new world in 3D where we have the power to create our own elements that we can keep for ourselves or share with others.

12. *Mathematics*: I really don't enjoy mathematics. In fact, I'm no good at it. What I do have is a drive and determination to get things done, and, when it comes to rigging, that means using mathematics. Luckily, calculators are readily available, so that's always helpful, and even with my useless math skills, I can persevere enough to create technical rigging setups. You need a reason to do math? Okay, how about scripting—you need it for that. You also need it to automate wheels turning, insects swarming, fish swimming, and wings flapping, and we need it for this book, as we need to automate movements through mathematics.

These rigging principles may not be as widely adopted as the principles of animation, but they're what I base my rigs on, and they form the most basic foundations for this book. Plus, they're a solid set of guidelines to keep us focused as we progress in our rigging journeys.

1.5 Naming Conventions

By default, each and every object created in 3D has a name. This name is assigned by the 3D software application as a basic way to identify an object individually. Usually, the names created are basic but specific. For instance, creating a Sphere in a new scene, it will be automatically named "Sphere01." Even if we start editing this object, the name will stay the same unless we manually change it.

This is totally fine, but if you have 700 *Spheres* in the same scene, it's pretty unlikely that we will know what each *Sphere* actually is or does, or where it is. This is where naming objects comes in particularly handy.

I stick to a very strict naming convention that I've been using for way too long. But, if it isn't broken, there's no need to fix it—so, I haven't! We'll be using this naming convention throughout this book, so it's a good idea to become familiar with it. However, it is not essential for you to stick rigidly to this; again, it's just a good guideline that has been tried and tested on numerous productions.

This naming convention covers five elements:

1. *Category*: The category of the object. This is required for each object.
2. *Item Name*: The actual name of the object. This is also a requirement.
3. *Number*: If it needs a number, this is where it goes.
4. *Side*: Left or right? Give it a side. This is optional, of course.
5. *Type*: What type of object is it? This is also required information.

We can combine these elements into a format that all objects in our scenes will use:

```
CATEGORY _ itemNameNumber _ SIDE _ TYPE
```

That's the basics of my naming convention, which we will be using in this book. If you're working in an actual production with others, you obviously have to be flexible and adaptable to the needs of the project. But, for this book, we'll be using the method outlined here. You're free to use your own, but if you're up for it, using my naming convention is what I'd suggest.

Here's a full breakdown of the naming convention so that you can get a better understanding of how things are going to work throughout this book (Table 1.1).

1.6 Layered Setups

Layered setups, also known as "layered rigging," is a methodology that I like to use when I create rigs. Think of four circles drawn around each other, each one bigger than the last. The outermost circle is the most important, as it is the circle that is always seen, yet because it is on the outside, it is the easiest circle to edit and change. As we move inward, each circle becomes more difficult to edit and change, and yet to the audience, they become less important, as they are not as easily seen (Figure 1.3).

Of course, the importance is from the viewpoint of the audience, as they can only see the outer circle. For us as riggers, all layers are equally important—after all, without the first layer, the second layer cannot be created or sustained, and so on. All layers need to work correctly, and they also need to work together to give a final result that is solid, stable, and intuitive. The final asset that appears on-screen needs to be believable to our audience, which wouldn't be possible if one of these layers fails.

1.7 3 Stage Asset Build (3SAB)

3SAB is another methodology that I rely on to make sure that things in a pipeline and on a schedule stick to their deadlines. At its most basic, this concept breaks down the creation of assets, no matter what they are, into three distinct stages:

1. Draft
2. Refinement
3. Polish

For instance, when modeling something, we can block it out quickly (stage 1). We can then move ahead and refine it by giving it the necessary details (stage 2).

Table 1.1 Naming Conventions

CATEGORY_itemNameNumber_SIDE_TYPE

CATEGORY (Required)

CAM	Camera
CH	Character
ENV	Environment
FX	Effect/Particle/Emitter
LI	Light
OBJ	Object or Prop
GUI	Graphical User Interface
GLOBAL	Shared by multiple categories

itemName (Required) [multiple]

Item names can be anything and everything that you want them to be. If you have more than one item name, use the minus (−) sign to split, but use this sparingly so that the item name length is reasonable.

itemNumber (Optional) [single]

Always use three (3) digits for item numbering. Example, *001*.

SIDE (Optional) [single]

If more clarity is needed, sides can be combined.

L	Left
R	Right
C	Center
LWR	Lower
UPR	Upper

TYPE (Required) [multiple]

ANIM	Animation
AS	Animation Set
AT	Animation Tree
BS	Blendshape/Morph Target
BRANCH	Second-Level Hierarchical Parent
CAM	Camera
CTRL	Controller
DATA	Data Node
GEO	Geometry
IK	Inverse Kinematic Chain
JNT	Joint/Bone
LI	Light
LINE	Spline/Curve/Line
LOC	Locator/Dummy/Point Helper
MAT_(D/N/S)	Material (Diffuse/Normal/Specular)

(Continued)

Table 1.1 (*Continued*) Naming Conventions

PA	Physics Asset
PFX	Particle System
RIG	Rigging Specific
ROOT	Hierarchical Parent (No other type suffix required)
TEMP	Temporary Item
UTIL	Utility Node

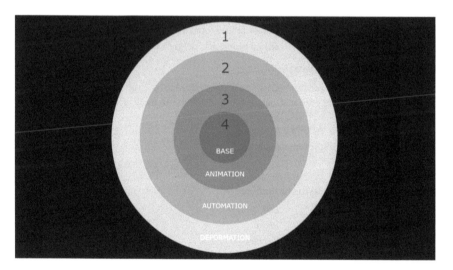

Figure 1.3

Layered setup rings of influence and importance.

At last, we can add the finishing touches and polish the model until it is complete (stage 3). For example, we can add this method to animation; the first thing we do is to block out the motion (stage 1), we can then spline the animation to smooth things out and make it close to final (stage 2), and then we can solidify all movements and add nuances by polishing (stage 3).

What's great about this methodology is that it gives us a breakdown of three specific sections, or goals that we can aim for. This iterative approach means that our work is constantly improving and we have smaller, more manageable stages to aim for, instead of just trying to complete something, which can be overwhelming at times. Additionally, it gives directors and supervisors the chance to give feedback, without destroying too much work if something needs changed. Best of all, once each stage is complete, we can send that section further into the pipeline for others to start using—meaning that projects and productions don't need to grind to a halt while other crew and team members are waiting for something to be completed.

When it comes to rigging, I like to break these three stages into the following divisions:

1. Base Rig
2. Animation/Automation Rig
3. Deformation Rig

This 3SAB approach can be used for every discipline in the production. Sometimes you have to be a little creative with it, but I find that it's a great way to think about the tasks at hand.

1.8 Colors

When it comes to using colors, we're free to do whatever we want. However, in an effort to keep things consistent, I like to use a specific color scheme that helps keep my rig creations similar and noticeable, and helps users become accustomed to what things they can interact with in my rigged scenes; it's also handy for giving visual representation of which side and component you are working with.

Borrowing from aircraft and maritime vehicles, I use red for any core control that is selectable on the left, and green for any core controller on the right. For core objects in the center, I use yellow. Additional core controllers are in blue, and extra controllers, which aren't part of the core systems, can be any color—I usually use white or purple.

Again, the option is up to you, but keeping a consistent color scheme, along with a consistent naming convention, is just good practice! (For more information, see Table 1.2.)

1.9 Companion Website

This book is designed so that you can create your own complex technical and mechanical setups using your own geometry and models. However, if you would like to work on the assets covered in this book, or if you would just like to check out anything that was created for the purposes of this book, then you need to go to the companion website and download the available resources (Figure 1.4).

Table 1.2 **Colors**

COLORS	
CENTER	Objects in the center
LEFT	Objects on the left
RIGHT	Objects on the right
ADDITIONAL	Extra objects that are part of the core element
EXTRA	Extra objects that are *not* part of the core element

Figure 1.4

The digital rigging companion website (www.digitalrigging.com).

You may notice other resources available on there too. These relate to other books on the topic of rigging, written by yours truly. Feel free to check out those assets too, and if you're interested, I can recommend the books to go along with them (of course!).

1.10 Memory Refresh

At the end of every chapter, and just before the Summary, which gives a brief overview of what was covered in the chapter, are "Memory Refresh" sections. These areas are designed to give you a place to quickly reference the key technical elements that have been covered in the chapter. This isn't so helpful for a first-time run-through of the book, but it certainly should be an area that you can reference at a later point, as well as for years to come!

For instance, this chapter has looked at websites, naming conventions, 12 principles, and layered setups. Therefore, the Memory Refresh is going to look something like what is shown in Table 1.3.

Table 1.3 **Memory Refresh: Introduction**

COMPANION WEBSITE

www.digitalrigging.com

OFFICIAL AUTODESK WEBSITE

www.autodesk.com

NAMING CONVENTIONS FORMAT

CATEGORY_itemNameNumber_SIDE_TYPE

12 RIGGING PRINCIPLES

1) KISS! – Keep It Simple, Stupid!

2) Planning

3) Research, Development, Resources

4) Anatomy

5) Biomechanics

6) Flesh-Surface Deformation

7) Animation

8) Modeling

9) Pipeline

10) Dynamics

11) Scripting

12) Mathematics

LAYERED SETUP STAGES

1) Base Rig

2) Animation/Automation Rig

3) Deformation Rig

3 STAGE ASSET BUILD (3SAB) STAGES

1) Draft

2) Refine

3) Polish

COLORS

CENTER
LEFT
RIGHT
ADDITIONAL
EXTRA

1.11 Summary

This chapter has served as an introduction to this book and the principles that are used throughout. By looking over the chapters that are upcoming, I hope that you have a better sense of where we're heading, and the plan that we'll be following throughout the text. If you've followed along successfully so far, you should have obtained some kind of 3D software and have an understanding of the naming conventions, color schemes, and general principles that we'll be using. You're also going to know the methodology that we cover when thinking of layered setups, and finally, you now know where to find the resources that we reference and use.

So, you know what we'll be covering, you know what preparations to take, and you know where the resources are located. It sounds to me like we're ready to start tackling the train.

2

Model

It all has to start somewhere, and without a model, we would have nothing to rig. We need an appealing model that has been created in such a specific way that the resulting geometry is suitable for the rigging tasks ahead. This is going to make our lives much easier when we start digging into the complicated areas of the setups that we're going to need to look at in order to complete this book.

Obviously, you can just skip all of these pages and look at the finished and final three-dimensional (3D) model of the steampunk train. In fact, if you scoot on over to the companion website (www.digitalrigging.com), you can get hold of the geometry, and even the completed rig itself. The thing is, before it got to that stage, a lot of work went into getting it there. When we first started, I literally had no idea what this thing was going to be or what it was going to look like. I mean, OK, I knew that it was going to be a steampunk-style locomotive, but that's about all the ideas and direction that I had at the time. I had some creative ideas floating around in my brain, but I really had no clue as to exactly what we were going to end up with in the end.

That said, this chapter is going to cover the model creation of the steampunk train that is now the main feature of this book. We're going to cover brainstorming and making notes from our ideas. Then we're going to look at the process of getting those ideas into the actual 3D model that will be used for the remainder of this book. We'll be using the 3 Stage Asset Build (3SAB) process for this, but we may have to bend the rules and be somewhat unconventional in order to get things done…you'll see what I mean as we progress through the chapters!

2.1 Conceptualization

Before starting work on any 3D model, and in this case the geometry of the steampunk train, we need to conceptualize the visuals, features, and elements featured in our completed model. Due to the complex and involved nature of these steampunk mechanics, we need to carefully assess what looks aesthetically appealing while keeping in mind the actual, practical functionality of the design itself.

Some things are obvious: It needs to look like a train—a steampunk train, no less. As is standard with trains, the first section, or carriage, should be the main carriage, the focal point and main feature of the locomotive. It should be the driving force that pulls the train powerfully forward; after all, that is where the engine will be located. Each coach needs to have wheels. These train wheels, also known as "rail wheels," need to be linked in some way, keeping closely to the style commonly associated with steam-powered trains. We're also going to need some kind of chimneys, exhausts, or both, which will be used to let out that big load of smoke that the locomotive engine is going to produce.

This should cover all the more obvious elements of the steampunk train design, but, for the not-so-obvious details, we have to dig a little deeper and really put our brains to work. We have to really focus on what we're going to include in our finished model, and for that, getting hold of some inspiration would be beneficial.

2.1.1 Reference

There is nothing new. There is nothing unique. Or at least that's what I've been told!

You see, it's all been done before, and what any of us create is usually a mixture of things that have inspired us and latched onto our conscious, subconscious, or some combination. A film, a TV show, a book, a video game, a poster, a story, a drawing, something online, an experience, anything and everything—the list goes on, and it all combines to influence our creative choices. These inspirational things can help and guide us as we create our own stuff. When it comes to the creation of a steampunk train, I know that I already have a number of visions I can recall, but it's going to be better to gather at least some reference that I can review, instead of just relying on my memory.

Gathering references is easy. A quick browse on the Internet and a search in your favorite search engine are all it takes. Getting hold of a good reference is harder. That Internet search turns into scanning websites and images for minutes, which eventually become hours. Getting a great reference is difficult. That simple search turns into looking at websites, looking at images, reading books, watching movies, visiting a museum—whatever it takes. And, after all of that, we need to collect all the references that are suitable into a location that can become our primary source of inspiration for future use on that particular project.

My reference gathering opened up a whole host of ideas that I'd like to incorporate into the steampunk train for this book. While spending time examining my collected references, I started to compile a list of all the visual features that could be included and that would be suitable for this project. Additionally, while browsing the reference that I had collected, my own creativity increased, so I started making a list of all the good ideas that came to mind, while throwing out the ideas that just weren't any good. To save you the hassle of trying to read and decipher my handwriting, here is a cleaned-up, edited, and compiled list that I will be referring to as I create the overall concepts for this locomotive. My buddy Chris also gets a copy of these notes so that he has a deeper understanding of the concepts and references as we move into the creation of the 3D assets.

Anyway, here's the list:

- *General Notes:*
    - Steampunk, as the name suggests, typically features steam-powered machinery in some kind of historical setting—which makes sense! However, it is also a specific genre of science fiction, and I'd really like to combine both historical and futuristic technologies into this design.
- *First/Main Carriage:*
    - The most important and most complex carriage.
    - This is the main feature of the train, including the engine, which pulls all the other carriages and coaches.
    - The main engine should include some kind of pistons that are both exposed and highly visible.
    - The engine should drive cogs, gears, and belts that can also be seen on the exterior of the train.
    - I'm thinking that something like the inner workings of an analog clock, or a watch, could look really great.
    - A chain should run from the visible cogs and gears. This would be the driving force for the wheels.
    - Perhaps some oversized wheels and some smaller ones would give a good contrast and style to this section.
    - Each wheel should have grooves that enable them to fit into the train tracks, and they should all be joined together so that they can be driven from the large wheel.
    - Do all of the wheels have to run on tracks? Maybe the large wheel could be something like a monster truck tire?!
    - The steam outlets, or exhausts should be retained at the top of the train. This will allow us to maintain that steam-powered style.

- *Second Carriage:*
  - This carriage needs to be connected to the First Carriage, but we should have a mechanism that allows it to be decoupled as needed.
  - It's common to have the Second Carriage store the fuel that the train engine will use in the First Carriage. In the case of a traditional steam engine, that would be a fossil fuel, coal. As I don't want to be too traditional with this design, and I'm trying to incorporate a futuristic spin on things, let's keep this carriage as the storage place for the fuel. But instead of coal, we can use a metallic container that can store various liquids and gases for this futuristic steampunk locomotive.
  - Pumps, tubes, and wires should connect the fuel containers to the First Carriage.
  - Standard train wheels should be linked and move as the carriage is pulled along, or we could use tiny wheels here for some added visual interest.
- *Third Carriage:*
  - Again, this carriage should include a latch that can couple and decouple the train.
  - The wheels are standard and connected.
  - Let's keep this carriage as a pretty standard and basic coach.
  - Maybe this is a storage carriage carrying…well, just carrying something that should be different and futuristic.
- *Fourth and Final Carriage:*
  - This is the public transport section.
  - A basic coach that carries passengers from A to B. You know, like a normal commuter train, but in an old-fashioned steampunk style.
  - Once more, this carriage will have standard and connected wheels. It will also include a latch for connecting and disconnecting this coach to and from the other carriages.
  - We should keep this carriage the most basic, as we already have so much going on in the other sections.
- *Track:*
  - A standard train track should suffice, but, depending on what we come up with, we could look into dual tracks or something equally crazy. OK, probably not, but it's something to think about for other projects, despite it probably not being practical.
- *Colors:*
  - Although I could not find any official steampunk colors, my references and research highlighted the use of earthly colors and a distinct lack of neon colors. It seems to be open season on which colors to use, which is great because it means that we get to choose pretty much whatever we want. I would like to combine historical and futuristic designs into this thing, so I'm going to experiment with muted blues, reds, greens,

grays, and gold as the main colors. This will be complimented with darker grays and some general dirt and grime. Of course, I say this now, but things could change!

Chris also had his own notes and several references that he had collected, and as he is the creator of the textures and geometry for this project, we ended up smashing our thoughts together to come up with a good middle ground. With these thoughts in notes, it's time to move on and start to scribble down these basic ideas into something more visual.

2.1.2 Scribbles and Concepts

This would be the perfect time for those super-artistic individuals out there to start scribbling and sketching out initial ideas in order to visualize the train. However, creating beautiful hand-drawn artwork is really not my thing—quick, raw, dirty, and definitely not pretty sketches are what I usually create. The thing is, as Chris and I are aligned on our vision already, and we have collected a great deal of amazing references, we can go ahead and skip creating this concept art and dive straight into the 3D modeling.

Of course, if you don't have the luxury of having references that drive the aesthetics, or if you're working on a large production team, you're going to need to create some form of concept art. Or if you're on the 3D team, concept art should be provided to you in order for you to keep your creative vision in line with what is needed for the project at hand.

2.2 Building the Model

Now that we have some direction in which we're going to take this model, we are ready to start building this steampunk train in 3D. It's no secret that I have the extremely talented Chris Rocks creating this model for me, not to be mistaken for the comedy genius "Chris Rock," even if Chris Rocks can be pretty hilarious at times. So, the following stages and discussions will use the progress that Chris and I make as we work together to create a model that is not only visually appealing, but also technically correct for the needs and specifications on this project.

2.2.1 Technical Considerations

Before rushing ahead, we need to think about and implement some basic technical stipulations. This will allow us to create a model that fits within predefined parameters and the overall scope of our project. With the output being intended for the use of this book, we're obviously free to come up with whatever we can imagine, the sky is the limit, but I'd like to keep things realistic.

The direct uses for this steampunk locomotive are for rigging tutorials, the front cover of this book, and short animation projects. In turn, these uses become the target platforms that have to be met. This means that we are creating the assets to run on prerendered output, but, if this rig were needed to run in a real-time rendering engine, then we really would need to create this rig with specifics that would allow it to run correctly. After all, your project may be for a video game or need real-time evaluation, so you may need to take into account other complexities that will stop the direct use of the train rig in this book working in a real-time engine—I'll do my best to highlight these sections that won't work as we go through the rigging process.

Scale for both scenes and objects can be troublesome, so agreeing and setting on a scale before we begin is the best idea. In fact, even the Autodesk 3ds Max instruction manual, or "Knowledge Network" as they like to call it, comes with a warning regarding the *Units Setup* of our scenes:

> Warning: Change the system unit value before you import or create geometry. Do not change the system unit in an existing scene.
>
> *Autodesk Knowledge Network*

Using real-world scales is my preferred method, and although my default thinking is to use the imperial feet and inches, I find that using metric units like millimeters, centimeters, and meters is a better option when working internationally—as we are in this book. So, that's what I'm going to go with for this train. I'll be setting my *Unit Setup* to *Meters*, and I'll be keeping my *Lighting Units* as *International*. However, setting these units is not enough. You see, by setting these, we simply change what is displayed to us—it is what we see as we interact with the interface, but it is not how 3ds Max calculates everything. To change the way that 3ds Max actually evaluates units, we have to edit the *System Unit Setup*, which we should set to *1 Unit = 1.0 centimeter* (Figure 2.1).

Once we have set these scale unit values, it is extremely important to keep these settings the same throughout the whole project, no matter what asset you may be working on. Trust me (if you don't already know)—changing these values once they have been previously set and are being used can lead to disaster for our scenes. It's a simple mistake that can be made, but fixing it is a big headache that we should attempt to avoid at all costs.

Setting and Changing Scene Units and System Units

For this project, we need to set our units to *Metric* and *Meters*, while we set our *Lighting Units* to *International*. Additionally, we need to make sure that our *System Unit Setup* equals *1 Unit = 1.0 Centimeters*.

```
CUSTOMIZE > UNITS SETUP > DISPLAY UNIT SCALE > METRIC > METERS
CUSTOMIZE > UNITS SETUP > LIGHTING UNITS > INTERNATIONAL
CUSTOMIZE > UNITS SETUP > SYSTEM UNIT SETUP > SYSTEM UNIT
SCALE > 1.0 > CENTIMETERS
```

* Make sure that the *Respect System Units in Files* checkbox is turned on (selected).

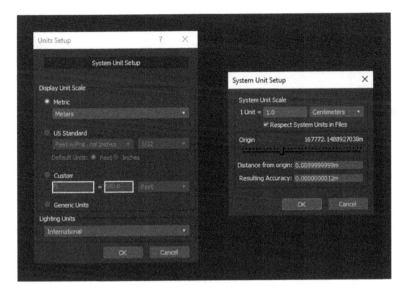

Figure 2.1

Units Setup and System Unit Setup with correct scales/unit calculations set.

The next thing that we have to think about is the triangle and polygon counts. Whether it be limited by a real-time video game engine, the fact that we have to rig this, or the desire to render this completed steampunk train, we have to come up with a restriction in order to make this a usable asset. I'm a big fan of keeping the geometry as light as possible and using the *Turbosmooth Modifier* to give the additional geometry needed to create smooth sides for rendering (if needed, of course). This is also helpful when thinking about assets created for video games. They need to be clean and light models that look great without a Turbosmooth! So, it makes sense that we should build to the standards of a high-end AAA video game, but to be able to increase the geometry density in certain areas if necessary. We can then add a *Turbosmooth Modifier* for any prerendered shots that may be needed, such as a book cover, publicity/marketing poster, and/ or a short animation sequence. Of course, as with any time, we add a *Turbosmooth Modifier*, we have to keep in mind that it will soften pretty much all edges—not a perfect situation for our hard-surface steampunk train. Luckily, we can just add "holding edges" to make sure that they keep their form and shape (Figure 2.2).

With all that said, we're going to be aiming for a maximum polygon count of 250,000 four-sided polygons. That's a total of around 62,500 per train carriage. Of course, more complex carriages can steal from carriages that don't need as much detail. But, overall, 250,000 is the upper limit for this asset. I have a feeling that we won't actually use that full amount of polygons, but it's better to be safe than sorry!

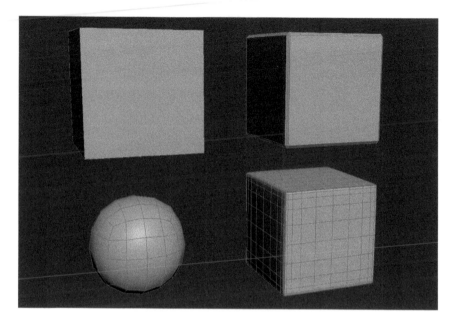

Figure 2.2

Holding edges literally hold the shape of objects when they are smoothed.

As you're working in 3ds Max, you can see the current amount of triangles and polygons in the scene by turning on *Statistics* for the viewport or by grabbing the *Polygon Counter* from the *Utilities Tab*.

Viewport Statistics and Polygon Counter Utility

You can get real-time statistics, feedback, and information from your scene, which includes polygon counts and triangle counts, by turning on viewport *Statistics*.

```
KEYBOARD BUTTON "7"
Or
VIEWPORT OPTIONS ([+]) > CONFIGURE VIEWPORTS... > STATISTICS >
  SHOW STATISTICS IN ACTIVE VIEW
Or
UTILITIES TAB > MORE... > POLYGON COUNTER
```

2.2.2 Rough Blocking

Stage 1 for modeling, using the 3SAB methodology, is Rough Blocking. It is here where Chris takes my notes, scribbles, and concept and starts to block out the rough steampunk train geometry. At this point, we're focusing on the rough form—shapes, sizes, dimensions. It is only when we're happy with the look and feel of the shapes do we go in and start to model with more accuracy during the Refinement phase.

By using a mixture of *Primitive Objects* to create the blocked-out shapes for this train, we're able to get something created in 3D that gives us an idea of how this is going to look. It's basic and it's not very pretty, but it is a start (Figure 2.3).

Most of the *Primitives* used in this basic model are *Boxes* that have been converted to an *Editable Poly*. Once converted, it is easy enough to drop into the *Sub-Object Level* and start tweaking and adjust into the shapes that are required. The thing is, although this is a start, both Chris and I did not like the way things were going. The great thing about keeping this so basic is that any changes or idea shifts that we had were not a big problem, and we could easily throw away any of these elements in favor of something different, as we weren't attached to any of this due to it being so rough.

We started to discuss other options for this train and decided to drop the huge wheels from the side, remove the front plow, and enhance the other carriages to make them more detailed and appealing. It's important to note that as Chris and I live in different countries often with different time zones, so we rely on a mixture of video chat, social media, and texting to stay in contact. This method of remote working is getting more and more popular, and when you think about it, why not?! For us, things actually work out really well this way; we've completed numerous successful projects by remote working—everything from TV commercials, to video games, to 3D book projects like this one.

As we agreed to push further into the blocking, changes were made and more detail was added. We were on the right track now, so we decided to make some technical decisions even at this early stage. For instance, we decided to make this train symmetrical. This means that Chris started to model only one side of the train, which sped up the modeling process, and actually all other processes in the future, such as texturing and rigging. These kinds of techniques are perfectly viable options. It all comes down to what is needed for the production and output.

Figure 2.3

Steampunk train blocking.

2.2.3 Refinement

With the blocking of the steampunk train now in a really great place, the model closely resembled the key form and factor of what we are trying to achieve, so Chris went ahead and started to detail each and every element that creates the train's overall composition. This includes the complex chains, cogs, sprockets, spring, suspension, connection…yeah, anything and everything, and it turned out to be a complex and challenging process. My words really don't do justice to how long these kinds of models can take, and this one certainly featured a very involved procedure, requiring lots of time and dedication. But at the end of the day, it's totally worth it to get a spectacular-looking 3D model (Figure 2.4).

It is also at this stage that we start thinking about the materials and textures that will be used in the final, polished model. This means that along with the refinement of the geometry, we start to both block in and then refine those materials and textures, working alongside and in parallel with the modeling tasks. I say "we," but Chris is responsible for all of this—he's the expert here, and his vision really drives the look of the locomotive forward.

We ended up using a lot of textures for this asset. If this model was aimed to run in a real-time game engine, there may be some issues with this, but as our target platform is prerendered for this book and any animation, we made the decision to use as many texture maps as we need, just so that things look as good as possible.

Special attention is also paid to the practicalities of the geometry. This means detailing the elements of the model, but not only for aesthetics—we're also detailing for movement and functionality. This is incredibly important, as not only does the train have to look visually amazing, it also has to look fantastic as motion (involuntary or automated changes) and movement (voluntary and

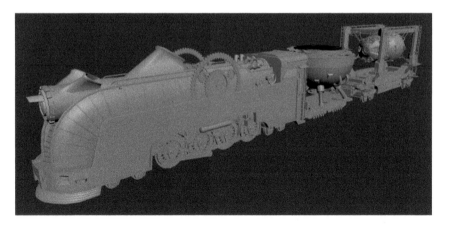

Figure 2.4

The refined steampunk locomotive starts to take on a shape that more closely represents how it will look when complete.

explicitly controlled changes) are applied to it via rigging and the process of animation. And, without carefully crafted geometry, no amount of skilled rig setups will cover up elements that fundamentally don't work together.

For clarity, when we jump into rigging this train, we are already using the final polished and complete model. This is done to keep things as readable as possible, with clear and concise instructions, but it is a luxury that we may not often have in a real-world production. In fact, if this were a project for film, TV, or games, it's possible that rigging would already be underway, and geometry replaced as newer versions become available. Crazy, but completely possible (even probable)!

Of course, with that said, there may be one or two issues from a modeling point of view that leak into the rigging process. These issues are kept to a minimum by good planning and skilled work, but they do happen at times. Sadly, there is no real way of spotting all errors and issues at this stage—you have to wait until it hits the rigging phase. If anything crops up here, we will fix it as we go, but things are looking great so far.

2.2.4 Polish

The model is just about complete, but as this is the final stage of 3SAB for modeling, it allows for any final/finishing touches, changes, fixes, and cleaning of the geometry, materials, and textures before it's time to call it a day! This is the final point for our geometry modeling where we can make adjustments and improvements, because when this is released into rigging, any and all changes have a big (and sometimes very destructive) effect. We can, of course, mitigate risks associated with geometric changes by using references and an iterative approach to our work, which we're already doing by using the 3SAB process. But things can always go wrong, so locking in the geometry at this stage is an important step to get right and can really make a big difference to a production.

Once again, Chris works hard to make sure that the geometry, materials, and textures are as good as they can be. This time, he is focusing his efforts on the smaller details and making sure that no further updates are needed. There are obviously many books and other resources out there to explain and guide you through the 3D modeling process if this is where you would like to spend more time, but this isn't that resource! We have to keep this train moving along so that we can get it into the rigging process where we're going to be spending most of our time. So, with that said, check out how stunning and detailed this finished 3D model of a steampunk train is (Figure 2.5)!

2.3 Naming of the Steampunk Locomotive

The Steampunk Train is a grand, detailed, and complicated piece of old-school, futuristic machinery. Now there's a juxtaposition for you! There are many elements that are combined to create this finished asset, but before we start digging into the technical aspects of setting this thing up for animation, let's take a moment to explore the model and come up with a name for this locomotive (Figure 2.6).

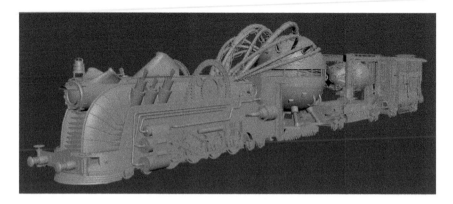

Figure 2.5

The finished 3D geometry, materials, and textures of the steampunk locomotive. There are many detailed elements that help to make this train very special.

Figure 2.6

The completed model and textures of the steampunk locomotive. It's pretty impressive!

Drum-roll please! Let's make this way more exciting than it actually is. We shall call this magnificent steampunk locomotive, none other than…

…Wait for it!…

NORAH.

That's what we'll call this train—Norah. I know, I know, what a spectacular name. Why call it this? I really don't know. It's just a name that came to me, and I thought that it suited it pretty well!

2.4 Memory Refresh

See Table 2.1.

Table 2.1 **Memory Refresh: Model**

SETTING AND CHANGING SCENE UNITS AND SYSTEM UNITS

CUSTOMIZE > UNITS SETUP > DISPLAY UNIT SCALE > METRIC > METERS
CUSTOMIZE > UNITS SETUP > LIGHTING UNITS > INTERNATIONAL
CUSTOMIZE > UNITS SETUP > SYSTEM UNIT SETUP > SYSTEM UNIT
  SCALE > 1.0 > CENTIMETERS

*Make sure the Respect System Units in Files checkbox is turned on (selected).

VIEWPORT STATISTICS AND POLYGON COUNTER UTILITY

KEYBOARD BUTTON "7"
Or
VIEWPORT OPTIONS ([+]) > CONFIGURE VIEWPORTS... > STATISTICS > SHOW
  STATISTICS IN ACTIVE VIEW
Or
UTILITIES TAB > MORE... > POLYGON COUNTER

2.5 Summary

We've covered a lot of topics in this section, from the initial idea generation to taking an in-depth look at the modeling process, including how everything fits together throughout the 3SAB process: (1) Rough Blocking, (2) Refinement, and (3) Polish.

During these modeling stages, we have created rough, even extremely primitive geometry, and then molded and sculpted these shapes into the final, rig-ready train, NORAH, that we can now take further into the production pipeline. We have exposed the exact processes and methods that both Chris and I have taken while working together on this asset. It's important to remember that we have been working together for a long time—we're talking years, not weeks or months! This has allowed us to find a harmony in our processes that can take a lot of time to achieve if you are part of a new team, group, or crew—but keep at it, and eventually everything just clicks into place.

I hope that this chapter has given you some food for thought when it comes to creating new models and assets, both for yourself and as part of a full team. Oh, and I have to say thank you once again to Chris. It was a challenge, but this turned out great.

3

Rigging Preparations

As with any newly created geometry, not everything is going to be perfect. Even if we were meticulous in our geometry creation, we really need to do some preparations before we jump in and start rigging. These preparations will end up drastically reducing complications further down the line, and although they require some effort, their implementation is not difficult by any means.

The payoff for taking the necessary time to go through all this preparation work is peace of mind, cleaner scenes, less chance of basic file issues or corruption, and clean, correctly named hierarchies and layers—the perfect way to start any rigging adventure. Some of the steps in this chapter will have to be repeated as we work through the three stages of the rigging process, but starting with the cleanest scene possible makes the endeavor the most worthwhile.

3.1 Model Breakdown

The very first order of business is a quick analysis of what we're going to be rigging. If this were a character, creature, or some kind of organic rig, this is where I'd spend time thinking about its anatomy and the biomechanics (to review these, please refer to the rigging principles found in Chapter 1, "Introduction"). With

NORAH being a steampunk locomotive, the model we're working with is hard-surface, inorganic geometry of the mechanical kind—at least for the most part. Still, we can approach things in a similar fashion to that of an organic model; we just adapt things a little bit.

I like to start things off by thinking about what kind of controls I'm going to need for the rig, where I'm going to place them, and what they are going to look like. Now, this can be just thoughts and rough ideas for now, but I have been known to take a few screenshots of the model, from various angles, allowing me to study each area and then sketch out where controllers are going to be needed. I'm not going to do that this time, but I do have some general thoughts on what I'm going to need, and it will be much more fun just to go ahead and create them as we go.

With that said, it's a good time to really look at this model in depth, and up close. Where are those possibly problematic areas? What things are definitely going to be challenging? Are there any areas that are a complete mystery to us in terms of how it can really work? Are there any details that are going to catch us off guard and/or require us to do some research into how best to enable movement and/or control over those details?

Our steampunk train, *Norah,* is a big challenge, but, here are my notes, which can give you an example of the kinds of things you should (or at least could) be thinking about:

- *NORAH—OVERVIEW OF POTENTIAL COMPLEXITIES*
  - GENERAL:
    - Automated wheel rotation for all carriages
    - Carriage linking
  - CARRIAGE 1:
    - Automated engine pistons
    - Automated side pistons
    - Front-bumper springs
    - Tube connections
  - CARRIAGE 2:
    - Tubes/hoses control
    - Automated fan rotations
    - Suspension springs
    - Suspension chains
    - Automated rumble/shake
  - CARRIAGE 3:
    - Suspension chains
    - Automated rumble/shake
  - CARRIAGE 4:
    - Nothing!

Researching possible solutions for these sections should be done right now, rather than later. It's a great point in the rigging process to isolate complex areas, create some temporary scenes and geometry that doesn't affect the main asset, and really work on coming up with practical and elegant solutions that we can transplant and reuse, or rebuild, on the actual rig later in the rigging process. The research and development of these difficult elements can often take a lot of time to complete, but spending time here will save us trouble later when we start to rig the finished geometry. For the purposes of this book, I'll leave any kind of prototyping until we start rigging the train itself as that's where we'll build the separated sections in isolation and add them into the core train rig afterward.

3.2 Redundant Geometry Removal

We have a few more steps to complete in order to clean both the model and the scene, making sure that everything is in top shape and ready for any rigging voodoo that we throw at it. Now, I'm pretty confident with the model that Chris has provided, but it doesn't hurt to take a quick look at the scene and also at the *Schematic View* to see if there is any geometry in the scene that has been left in there by accident. So, go on, what are you waiting for? Go take a look at those places and see what you find. If there is any redundant geometry or objects, clear them out—if it's not going to be part of the rigged model, it's just not needed. Oh yeah, I should mention that if you notice any construction elements, such as *Splines*, that are part of how the geometry has been created, you have to go in there and make sure that you correctly collapse the *Modifier Stack* before deleting anything. This will prevent any undesirable effects that may appear if you simply delete objects that are part of the foundation of the geometry. There is no need to worry about the geometry of our steampunk train, *NORAH*, as I've made sure that's already completely clean for you to work on.

Collapsing the Modifier Stack

If you have multiple *Modifiers* in the *Modifier Stack*, we can always collapse everything down, effectively cleaning out the *Modifiers*, but retaining their effects on the geometry. This technique works great for many situations, but it does eliminate any interactive *Modifiers*, so that further changes cannot be made easily.

```
[SELECT GEOMETRY] > [RIGHT-CLICK GEOMETRY] > CONVERT
TO: > CONVERT TO EDITABLE POLY
```

For an asset like *NORAH*, this can be a time-consuming process. Although it is not particularly challenging, it is important to keep focused, which is sometimes easier said than done.

3.3 Setting the Scale

As with any scene, one of the most important things to check is that the correct units are being used. This was covered in the previous chapter, so you should be good to go. But if you need a review, check the "Memory Refresh" section in that chapter. Remember that we're setting the *Display Unit Scale* to *Metric* and *Meters*, with the *Lighting Units* set to *International*. The *System Unit Setup* should be *1 Unit = 1.0 Centimeters*.

Things might look great at this point, but we now need to check to see if the assets we've been provided with are at the correct scale. I've found that the best way of doing this is to have some kind of human representation in the scene. By adding a generic human, we can easily see if the scale of objects in the scene is proportional to us as humans. For instance, a door should be tall enough and wide enough for a human to go through, unless there is some specific reason otherwise. Likewise, a sofa should be easy to sit on, with no need to climb onto it!

Adding in a generic human simply allows us to check to see that the size of objects is correct and ergonomically accurate. For me, the simplest way of getting some kind of human representation within our scenes is to create a *Biped*. And if we set the *Biped* to a height of *1.828 meters (6 foot)*, we get a pretty good depiction that we can use as our reference.

Biped Creation

Use a *Biped* with a height of *1.828 meters (6 foot)* to give a very fast visual representation of a generic human.

```
CREATE TAB > SYSTEMS > STANDARD > BIPED
```

This should give you great visual feedback for the size of a typical human, and you should be able to instantly tell if anything just doesn't look all right. Then again, even if things look great, we can use the *Tape* tool to measure distances and scales of things in the scene. It's worth spending time doing this so that the default sizes for your rig are going to be usable straight away (Figure 3.1).

Creating a Tape

Create a *Tape* to accurately measure elements within your scene.

```
CREATE TAB > HELPERS > STANDARD > TAPE
```

Now I'm no expert in railways, trains, locomotives, or whatever, but I think that these steam-powered trains are pretty huge. So, a quick Internet search for "dimensions of a steam train" got a few results. In particular, the "Union Pacific

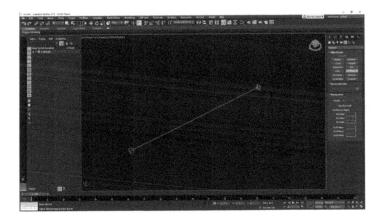

Figure 3.1

The *Tape* tool is a great way to give a visual representation of size within our scenes.

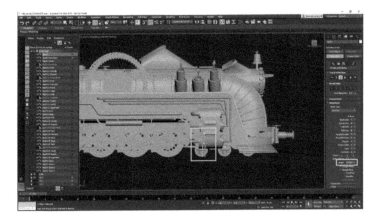

Figure 3.2

The size of the steampunk train, *NORAH*, in comparison to a generic human (see green boxes).

Big Boy," which according to Wikipedia* was manufactured between 1941 and 1944 and operated until 1959, stood at around 4.94 meters (16 foot 2 inches, or thereabouts). OK, so pretty big!

NORAH should be just as tall—in fact, it should be taller because this is a futuristic steampunk machine! So, we need to measure out a *Tape* tool that reads *10 meters* (around *32.8 feet*), I know, this is huge. This allows us to scale up the train in *XYZ* until the tallest part matches the height of the measured-out *Tape* (Figure 3.2).

---

* Wikipedia, s.v. "Union Pacific Big Boy," last modified October 24, 2018, https://en.wikipedia.org/w/index.php?title=Union_Pacific_Big_Boy&oldid=864248478.

3.4 Geometry and Wireframe Colors (Optional)

Admittedly, this has become a kind of ritual for me, and it is a completely optional step to take, but I like to change the colors of the geometry and the wireframe display. Of course, I don't do this for fun—let's face it, it isn't really fun at all! But changing these colors helps me work faster and is specifically useful for when we get into skinning, as it creates a nice neutral tone so that the colors of the weighting data can be distinguished easily. I like to use a *gray* for the geometry and a *black* for the selection—but as it doesn't affect the workings of Autodesk 3ds Max, just choose colors that you like to work with.

Change Object and Wireframe Color

This is a completely optional step, but one that can make scene objects very neutral so that we're not distracted.

```
[SELECT OBJECT] > CREATE PANEL > NAME AND COLOR > COLOR
SWATCH > [Gray]

CUSTOMIZE > CUSTOMIZE USER INTERFACE... > COLORS > ELEMENTS:
GEOMETRY > SELECTION > [Black]
```

3.5 Name, Names, and Naming

With the optional colors set, we must go on to the (unfortunately) extremely dull task of making sure that each and every geometry object is named correctly. I know, it's boring and tedious, but it's super-important, so there's no getting out of it. We can't rely on our models being named correctly when we receive them, as it's our job to make sure that this is all correct. After all, it affects us the most as we go into the rigging stages.

Obviously, I'll be using the predefined naming structure that I mentioned earlier; for instance, a wheel will use the following name:

OBJ_norah1Wheel001_L_GEO

A piston from the engine will be:

OBJ_norah1Piston001_R_GEO

A cog will be:

OBJ_norah1Cog_GEO

And the last carriage will be:

OBJ_norah4Carriage_GEO

That should make naming the rest of the geometry pretty obvious and logical. It takes some time to make sure that everything is named correctly, but the effort is always worthwhile.

3.6 Creating the Geometry Hierarchy

Creating hierarchies is creating the structure that supports all elements in the rigging world! So, let's get started with the geometry. I use groups, and those groups literally put things together, but it's important to note that I'm not using the *Groups* in the 3ds Max toolset. At its most basic, these group nodes that I create here are simply an object in which to parent other objects. I should clarify again, I don't use the grouping tool found on the *Main Menu* of 3ds Max ([SELECT OBJECTS] > MAIN MENU > GROUP > GROUP...), at least not for rigging purposes.

Point Helpers are what we're going to use as our group nodes. These *Point Helpers* are pretty much the exact same thing as a *Dummy* object, but, they have the added advantage of being able to have a few visual display options. Which options you choose are just your personal preference, but it's a nice addition to have rather than using a *Dummy* object (Figure 3.3).

As a starting point, we need to create a *Point Helper*, positioned at the center of the scene (*XYZ[0,0,0]*), and in this case, it is named "*OBJ_norah_GEO_GRP.*" Then it's as simple as grabbing all the geometry and using the *Select and Link* tool to link them (or in other words, parent them) to the created group Node—the *Point Helper.*

Create Geometry Group

A geometry group, or in fact any group, is a number of nodes parented under a *Point Helper.*

CREATE TAB > HELPERS > STANDARD > POINT

Move "Point001" to XYZ[0,0,0]
Rename "Point001" to "OBJ_norah_GEO_GRP"
Use the *Select and Link* tool to parent the geometry to "OBJ_norah_ GEO_GRP"

With the geometry now sitting under one group, we could just leave things like that, but, as *NORAH* is comprised of many objects, we should really continue to group the geometry into separate elements. This won't help us right now, but when we come to the next chapter and we tackle the Base Rig, we'll be grateful that we bothered to group the geometry into clear and specific grouped elements.

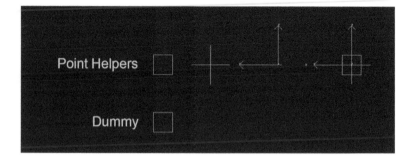

Figure 3.3

Visual differences between *Point Helpers* and *Dummy* objects.

There are four sections, or carriages, to the train, so by using four *Point Helpers*, we have to create a geometry group ("*GEO_GRP*") for each important part. Of course, these should be sitting in the center of the scene at *XYZ[0,0,0]*, and named as follows:

- OBJ_norah1_GEO_GRP
- OBJ_norah2_GEO_GRP
- OBJ_norah3_GEO_GRP
- OBJ_norah4_GEO_GRP

I'm denoting each section of the train with a number, just for clarity and ease of naming. Hey, you can't blame me for taking a shortcut after all that naming we just did previously for each part of the geometry. Additionally, I'll be quickly grouping each part of the train, using the *Group* options in 3ds Max, just so that I can center each carriage of the train. This makes all the geometry overlap, but as we'll be working on each section separately, this makes a lot of sense. At the very end, we'll join everything together and make it all look pretty once again.

So, you probably already guessed this, but we now need to parent the geometry of *NORAH* under each of the respective *Point Helpers*. There isn't any tricks here, just plain old making hierarchies. With everything sitting under their own groups, simply parent them under the *OBJ_norah_GEO_GRP*, and we're good to go! (Figure 3.4).

3.7 Resetting and Aligning Pivots

I like to reset the pivot point of each geometry object so that it is aligned to the world and sits in the center of the scene, at *XYZ[0,0,0]*. This might seem illogical or counterintuitive to those that use the pivot points of objects as a location for transformations, such as rotating. In fact, parenting geometry elements together and then rotating them via their pivot points is a perfectly fine way of rigging something. However, I've had issues with directly changing the transform

Figure 3.4

Geometry elements correctly grouped and parented under the *OBJ_norah_ GEO_GRP*.

properties of geometry, and for real-time game engines, this may be very problematic. So I stick with centering the pivots of any geometry I get and using some other object, such as a *Point Helper, Dummy,* or *Bones* as the thing that I use to transform the geometry indirectly—even when the asset won't be going into a real-time rendering engine…after all, you never know what the future will have in store for the rigs that we are creating.

Align *Pivots* to *World* and Move to *Scene Center*

Pivot Points can be super-helpful, but as they are related to an object's transform, they can become a nightmare. It's often better to just align pivots to the world and move the location of the pivots to the center of the scene.

HIERARCHY TAB > PIVOT > AFFECT PIVOT ONLY > ALIGN TO WORLD

HIERARCHY TAB > PIVOT > AFFECT PIVOT ONLY > X = 0, Y = 0, Z = 0

Now that we've edited each object's pivot, we have definitely messed up something on each object's transform. Of course, these could have been broken during the modeling, but it's a good opportunity to fix things anyway. Let's do that right now...

3.8 Reset the Transforms

To fix the transforms of our objects, we can simply use one of the tools built into 3ds Max—the *Reset XForm* tool. *Reset XForm* removes all *Rotation* and *Scale* values from selected objects and places those transforms in an *XForm* modifier. By resetting the transforms, we reset the object's transformational data and in fact clean the object up for further use! Sometimes this causes the *normals* of the geometry to flip, but by adding a *Normal Modifier,* we can fix this up quickly.

With these steps complete, we have to remember to collapse them down and convert the geometry to an *Editable Poly*. It's important to then finish these edits by freezing the transforms. This will finish cleaning up the geometry, making it solid and safe for rigging.

Reset Geometry and Reset Transforms

This is an important step to do before rigging any geometry. Often when creating, building, editing, and manipulating geometry, object data can become corrupted. Not only will this remove any garbage that has been inadvertently stored in the model, but it also can stop potential problems from happening later in the production process.

[SELECT GEOMETRY] > UTILITIES TAB > RESET XFORM > RESET SELECTED

(Optional) (If needed) [SELECT GEOMETRY] > MODIFY TAB > MODIFIERS > NORMAL

[SELECT GEOMETRY] > [RIGHT-CLICK GEOMETRY] > CONVERT TO: > CONVERT TO EDITABLE POLY

[Select Geometry] > [Alt and Right-Click] > FREEZE TRANSFORM > YES

Our geometry is now clean, grouped correctly, and ready for rigging. This is a good time to make sure that the scene itself is cleaned appropriately so that it will be as stable as possible when we start rigging.

3.9 Cleaning up the Scene

Technically, our scene and geometry are already pretty much clean. But it wouldn't be the first time that I thought everything was cleaned up and ready for rigging, just to find out a few hours later that I was very wrong! This can happen for a number of reasons, and it's just one of those things that just sometimes can't be prevented. However, I have a few steps that I have found can help to reduce possible issues as we develop our rig and move past rigging and into animation and other departments.

These steps are really simple—we first need to save out our geometry to a new file. To do this, simply select the geometry groups, as well as all the geometry, and then use the *Save Selected* option from the *File* menu so that only the specific nodes that have been selected manually are saved into a new scene.

With a new file saved, we can go ahead and reset 3ds Max. From there, we can then *Merge* that saved scene into the newly reset, super-clean scene! Finally, we can use the *Save As* option and save the file with the appropriate name.

Following all these steps gives us the cleanest possible file we can get. It removes any extra nodes, calculations, and general garbage that may have been inadvertently stored in the scenes that we have been working on up to this point.

Creating a Clean and Stable Scene

These few steps, which are insanely simple, should give you the cleanest and most stable scene ever!

```
FILE > SAVE SELECTED... > [Create a saved.max file with
  appropriate naming.]

FILE > RESET

FILE > IMPORT > MERGE > [Select saved scene] > ALL

FILE > SAVE AS... > [Overwrite the previously saved file and use
  the same file name]
```

3.10 Setting the Display Layers (Layers Explorer)

We only have one more thing left to do, and that is to create specific *Display Layers* that are not only going to be useful for rigging, but also be beneficial to us for organizational purposes, or anyone else using our rig once it is fully complete. To create new *Display Layers*, click on the *Toggle Layer Explorer* found on the *Main Toolbar*. This will open a floating window named *Scene Explorer—Layer Explorer*.

In this new window, one display layer will already be created for us. This display layer is always named *0 (default)*. We need to add to this and create a number of other layers with the following names and uses:

- 0 (Default)
  - Automatically created by 3ds Max. Just leave it alone!
- ANIM
  - Used for animation-specific data.
- BS
  - BS stands for *Blendshapes*, a term used in Autodesk Maya that refers directly to *Morph Targets* in 3ds Max. I know, I should probably change this, but I'm so used to it that it has now become kind of a tradition!
- CAM
  - Cameras! Any and all kinds of them go in here.
- CTRL
  - Short for "controls" or "controllers." This is where we will put the animatable controls of our rigs.
- DATA
  - Nodes that hold attributes or specific data information are stored in this layer.
- DEFORM
  - Deformation nodes sit in this layer.
- FX
  - Effects objects and emitters go in here.
- GEO
  - All geometry should be placed in this layer.
- LI
  - Lights used to illuminate the scene and its objects reside in here.
- MSCLE
  - Muscles! Although these are technically deformation nodes, we keep them separate so that they are easier to find, as things can often become complicated in technical rigs.
- RIG
  - All rigging-related nodes that don't fit into the other layers should be placed in this layer.
- SKEL
  - This is the closet for all your skeletons!
- WIP
  - This is the "work in progress" layer. It's here where we will be storing everything as we develop things, before moving completed work into the other layers.

With the new *Display Layers* created, grab all the geometry and the geometry groups in the scene. Add them to the *GEO Display Layer* by first selecting the *GEO* layer, and then pressing the *Add to Active Layer* button (Figure 3.5).

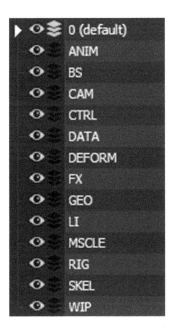

Figure 3.5

Shown here are the display layers that will be used during the development of our steampunk locomotive rig.

Creating Display Layers and Assigning Objects

The *Layer Explorer* allows use to create, edit and delete display layers and their associated objects and properties. This *Layer Explorer* is a version of the *Scene Explorer* that is specifically configured for managing layers, although you can manage layers from any other *Scene Explorer* if you wish.

MAIN TOOLBAR > TOGGLE LAYER EXPLORER

Or

LAYERS TOOLBAR > TOGGLE LAYER EXPLORER

Or

ENHANCED MENU: SCENE MENU > MANAGE SCENE CONTENTS > LAYER
 EXPLORER

Or

SCENE EXPLORER > VIEW TOOLBAR > DROP-DOWN LIST > LAYER EXPLORER

That's it! Save your scene and take a break. We've just finished up the preparations needed to start rigging this steampunk locomotive, and we're in a great place to start thinking about the *Base Rig* and any common rigging techniques that we will need to use in order to create a solid and stable rig that's ready for animation.

3.11 Memory Refresh

See Table 3.1.

Table 3.1 **Memory Refresh: Rigging Preparations**

COLLAPSING THE MODIFIER STACK

```
[SELECT GEOMETRY] > [RIGHT-CLICK GEOMETRY] > CONVERT TO: > CONVERT
 TO EDITABLE POLY
```

BIPED CREATION

```
CREATE TAB > SYSTEMS > STANDARD > BIPD
```

CREATING A TAPE

```
CREATE TAB > HELPERS > STANDARD > TAPE
```

CHANGE OBJECT AND WIREFRAME COLOR

```
[SELECT OBJECT] > CREATE PANEL > NAME AND COLOR > COLOR SWATCH
 CUSTOMIZE > COLORS > ELEMENTS: GEOMETRY > SELECTION
```

ALIGN PIVOTS TO WORLD AND MOVE TO SCENE CENTER

```
HIERARCHY TAB > PIVOT > AFFECT PIVOT ONLY > ALIGN TO WORLD
HIERARCHY TAB > PIVOT > AFFECT PIVOT ONLY > X = 0, Y = 0, Z = 0
```

RESET GEOMETRY AND RESET TRANSFORMS

```
[SELECT GEOMETRY] > UTILITIES TAB > RESET XFORM > RESET SELECTED
(Optional) (If needed) [SELECT GEOMETRY] > MODIFY
 TAB > MODIFIERS > NORMAL
[SELECT GEOMETRY] > [RIGHT-CLICK GEOMETRY] > CONVERT TO: > CONVERT
 TO EDITABLE POLY
[Select Geometry] > [Alt & Right-Click] > FREEZE TRANSFORM > YES
```

CREATING A CLEAN AND STABLE SCENE

```
FILE > SAVE SELECTED... > [Create a saved.max file with appropriate
 naming.]
FILE > RESET
FILE > MERGE > [Select saved scene]
FILE > SAVE AS... > [Overwrite the previously saved file and use the
 same file name]
```

CREATING DISPLAY LAYERS AND ASSIGNING OBJECTS

```
MAIN TOOLBAR > TOGGLE LAYER EXPLORER
Or
LAYERS TOOLBAR > TOGGLE LAYER EXPLORER
Or
ENHANCED MENU: SCENE MENU > MANAGE SCENE CONTENTS > LAYER EXPLORER
Or
SCENE EXPLORER > VIEW TOOLBAR > DROP-DOWN LIST > LAYER EXPLORER
```

(Continued)

Table 3.1 (*Continued*) Memory Refresh: Rigging Preparations

DISPLAY LAYERS
```
0(default)
ANIM
BS
CAM
CTRL
DATA
DEFORM
FX
GEO
LI
MSCLE
RIG
WIP
```

3.12 Summary

This chapter has covered some very simple and easy steps that allow us to have a super-clean 3ds Max scene that we can use for our rig with confidence. Each and every one of the rigs that I produce goes through this same routine, and as you now know, it requires only a small amount of time and effort. For the time and effort that we put into this stage of the rigging process, we get a scene file that is as clean as possible. With this file in place, and with the rigging preparations now complete, we can focus our attention to the core foundations of the *Base Rig* without needing to worry if there is anything that we have missed. This scene should be as stable as it can be, so let us start creating the *Base Rig*.

You can find the completed model, which includes all finished stages from this chapter, in the supporting file:

OBJ_norah_GEO.max

4

Common Rigging Techniques

Admittedly, I debated over whether this chapter was actually needed in this book. After all, we're rigging a complex and technical steampunk locomotive, so I'm presuming that you're already aware of all of the rigging techniques and methods that are commonly used. But I figured that we should go over them anyway. You never know, there might be another tool in here that you don't often use and could use a review of, or a basic tool that you don't often use and that I might utilize in a different way!

It doesn't matter now—this chapter is here to stay, and we'll be looking at creating controllers and wiring parameters, among other topics. Although not put into practical use just yet, this is a great stage to really get to grips with and understand these tools and processes, as we will be using these techniques multiple times in the upcoming chapters to create the finished *NORAH* rig.

These common techniques are widely used when rigging anything from characters to beasts, and from crowds to cars. These tools and methods are relatively standard practices when rigging assets in three dimensions (3D). I'm introducing these things now, as not only will they give us time to get used to the steps required to create them, but we won't have to keep repeating the same steps over and over. If we kept going over things, it would be boring, right?! Like, really boring!

As we're going over these practical methodologies within this chapter, the following chapters will simply refer to them by name, instead of repeating the same instructions over and over again (trust me, it would be super-boring if I spent this whole book repeating the same basic steps), so be sure to keep them locked up in your memory vault of awesomeness!

4.1 Hierarchies

Possibly the most useful tool when rigging in Autodesk 3ds Max, or in any 3D software, is the ability to link objects to one another. This forms a chain, a hierarchical structure in which the linked object, known as the *Child*, inherits the transformations of the object that it is linked to, known as the *Parent*. Sometimes these relationships are known as the *Slave* and *Driver*, respectively. But whatever you call them, these parent-and-child hierarchy relationships can be overly simple or relatively complex, depending on the needs of the rig.

Creating hierarchies is a very simple task. By using the *Select and Link* tool found on the *Main Toolbar*, we can link objects by using the left mouse button to click-and-drag one object to another (Figure 4.1).

To view hierarchies within our 3ds Max scenes, we can use the *Scene Explorer*, which is also found on the *Main Toolbar*. However, I prefer to use the *Schematic View*, which, in my opinion, gives a clearer view of a scene's hierarchies and even allows editing of hierarchies. I highly recommend taking a look at the *Schematic View* and taking the time to learn how it works, as it can make working with complex rigs much easier (Figure 4.2).

4.2 Skeletons

If this were an organic rig, we would be using *Bones* and the *Bone Tools* to create digital skeletons that form the foundations for the articulation of our rigs. However, as *NORAH* is a huge, hard-surfaced mechanical steampunk locomotive, creating a skeleton is completely optional (actually, it is always optional, but we

Figure 4.1

The *Select and Link* tool is easily found on the *Main Toolbar*.

4. Common Rigging Techniques

Figure 4.2

The *Scene Explorer* and the *Schematic View* show the hierarchies within an open scene, and both are accessible from the *Main Toolbar*.

won't get into that here). Of course, this doesn't mean that we can't use *Bones* to help with our rigging; it just means that a skeleton won't be the dominant infrastructure that will support our rigs.

Creating and Editing *Bones*

Bones may not form the foundation of our hard-surface rig at this time, but they are still incredibly useful tools that we can exploit to our advantage.

```
CREATE TAB > SYSTEMS > STANDARD > BONES
```

Or

```
ANIMATION MENU > BONE TOOLS ...
```

Bones can be a very useful tool for many rigging situations, and the way in which *Bones* are linked mean that they form a *Forward Kinematic* chain. These *Forward Kinematics* also can be converted into *Inverse Kinematics* if necessary…

4.3 Forward and Inverse Kinematics

Usually associated with *Bones*, *Forward Kinematics (FK)* and *Inverse Kinematics (IK)* are terms used to describe the articulation of a hierarchical structure. *FK* is the simplest to understand, and we gain automatic control of *FK* chains as we create hierarchies; the rotation of a parent affects the children, and so on down the chain, a top-down methodology. *IK* is the opposite of this—it allows us to control the hierarchical chain from the lowest child, a bottom-up methodology (Figure 4.3).

As already mentioned, *FK* is available for free, but *IK* requires us to work for it (but not too much)! By adding a *HI Solver IK* chain to a bone chain or a hierarchy of objects, we are able to control those objects via *IK*.

Adding Inverse Kinematics to *Bones* and Hierarchies

The first thing that you need is a hierarchy of objects and/or a *Bone* chain. With those elements already in place, select the parent object, and then add the *HI Solver IK* chain.

```
[SELECT PARENT IN HIERARCHY] > ANIMATION MENU > IK SOLVERS > HI
SOLVER
```

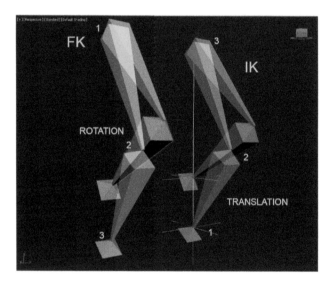

Figure 4.3

The control differences between *FK* and *IK*.

4. Common Rigging Techniques

You probably noticed that there are another three *IK Solvers* in the list where we chose the *HI Solver*. These other *IK Solvers*—the *HD Solver*, the *IK Limb Solver*, and the *SplineIK Solver*—all have their uses, but I'll leave the choice to you if you'd like to take some time experimenting with them before we move on!

4.4 Skinning

Skin, or *Skinning,* is a built-in tool that allows us to deform one object with another. This is most commonly associated with skeletal deformations, where we use *Bone* objects to deform the geometry of a model, and it works exactly the same way as our real-world skeletons (bones) deform our real-world bodies (skin).

Skinning is a basic topic that requires patience and practice to master. There are also some other steps that can improve the skinned mesh, such as *Angle Deformers* or *Pose-Space Deformers* and *Dual-Quaternion Skinning*, among many others. We will need to skin elements of our steampunk locomotive, so it's best to familiarize yourself with at least the most basic skinning procedures before progressing. Refer to the 3ds Max manual for detailed information and tutorials on how to use the *Skin Modifier.*

Skinning and the *Skin Deformer*

Skinning of geometry is more common with organic models and rigs, but we shouldn't forget about this powerful deformer while we create rigs for hard-surface models. To skin geometry, we first need some geometry and a *Bone* chain (it could be a different kind of object if you want to be adventurous) in our scene, and then we can add the *Skin Modifier* …

```
[SELECT OBJECT FOR SKINNING] > MODIFY TAB > MODIFIER LIST >
OBJECT-SPACE MODIFIERS > SKIN

Or

[SELECT OBJECT FOR SKINNING] > MODIFIERS MENU > ANIMATION > SKIN
```

It's important to note that the *Skin Modifier* can be used with any object within 3ds Max. This means that literally anything that we create can influence another object with this tool—it doesn't just have to be *Bone* objects. This can be very helpful and is somewhat different from other 3D applications, as they force you to use *Bones,* also known as *Joints,* with their skinning tools.

4.5 Constraints

Constraints are a special type of *transform controller* (more on those a bit later in this chapter) that can automate the control of an object's *position, rotation,* or *scale.* There are many common uses for using a *constraint,* and they are used continuously when it comes to animation, as they are extremely helpful for linking one object to another (or many objects) in a variety of ways. Once a *constraint* has been set, an animator can use *keyframes* to toggle its binding relationship over a period of time.

Adding *Constraints*

Creating a *constraint* is simple. Remember to select the object that you want constrained first.

```
[SELECT OBJECT] > ANIMATION MENU > CONSTRAINTS > [ANY OPTION]
```

4.6 Controllers

When I mention "controllers," I"m usually referring to the controls that an animator can take hold of and manipulate. You know, the kinds of controllers that you see surrounding characters and objects on most rigs (Figure 4.4).

The thing is, animation in 3ds Max is performed through *transform controllers*. Most commonly, we can think about the *transform controllers* that we have access

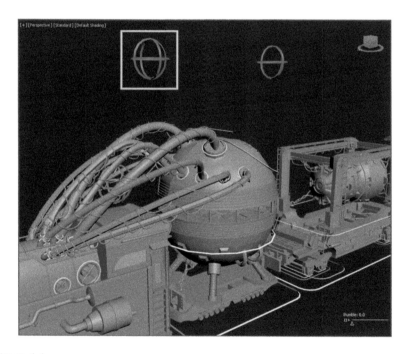

Figure 4.4

Controls/controllers for animators to animate.

to when we create a new object—the *move (position)*, *rotate*, and *scale* controllers. Each *animation track* is actually assigned its own *transform controller*, and each *transform controller* can be completely different, or even combined. In fact, by using constraints as we did just before, we actually assigned a new *transform controller* to the objects that we constrain. If this is sounding a little weird to you right now, don't worry. Let's work through this section and figure out what these differences really are.

4.6.1 Interactive Viewport Controllers (Animation)

Controllers that animators use to manipulate your rig can be anything you want them to be. Personally, I prefer to use a *Spline* object for most of the controllers that are in the *Viewports*. These are easy to create, can have their visibility easily adjusted, and are great to style and edit as needed. You can create a *Spline* controller by heading on over to the *Create Tab*, jumping into the *Shapes* options, and by making sure that *Splines* is selected in the drop-down menu.

Creating Viewport Controllers

The controllers that we are going to use during the creation of the steampunk train rig are spline objects. They are easy to create, easy to edit, and easy to evaluate quickly in the viewports.

CREATE TAB > SHAPES > SPLINES > [ANY OPTION]

There are already a number of premade shapes to choose among in this creation menu, and I usually stick with a *Line*, *Rectangle*, or *Circle* as my core controller shapes. Of these, the *Line* is the most versatile, as it is very easy to use to draw custom shapes. Once a controller has been created, such as a *Spline Circle*, we can head on over to the *Modify Tab* to adjust how it visually appears in the *Viewports* (Figure 4.5).

With the *Spline* shape controller selected, we can use the *Enable In Viewport* option, found under the *Rendering Rollout*, to give it an appealing look in the viewport. However, by doing this, we're causing 3ds Max to actually draw, or render, the object within the *viewport*. This is not a problem right now, but as we keep adding rigging or other objects into this scene, things can start to slow down, which is not a good thing at all. To enable us to get the maximum speed from our viewports, as well as enable the rendering of the *Spline* controllers, we can change the number of rendered *Sides* to *three (3)*. Additionally, under the *Interpolation Rollout*, changing the *Steps* to *three (3)* also helps with the viewport speed. Both of these changes affect the look of our controllers, but not enough to have a real negative impact to their aesthetics.

Figure 4.5

The various *Spline* object styles and options available for free.

Enabling Viewport Rendering of Controller Objects

If you'd like to add some visual flair to your controllers, simply turn on the rendering in the viewport option. Just remember to adjust the number of *Sides* and *Interpolation* to *three (3)* so that they render quickly in the viewport.

```
[SELECT SPLINE CONTROLLER] > MODIFY TAB > RENDERING > ENABLE IN
VIEWPORT > ON

[SELECT SPLINE CONTROLLER] > MODIFY TAB > RENDERING > SIDES > 3

[SELECT SPLINE CONTROLLER] > MODIFY TAB > INTERPOLATION > STEPS > 3
```

One final thing that we can do is combine these shapes so that we can create truly unique controllers. To do this, right-click on your *Spline* controller and convert the *Shape* to an *Editable Spline*. After that, click the *Attach* button, found under the *Geometry Menu,* and select another *Shape* in the scene. This will combine both shapes into an *Editable Spline* and leave us with a pretty great and visually appealing controller (Figure 4.6).

4. Common Rigging Techniques

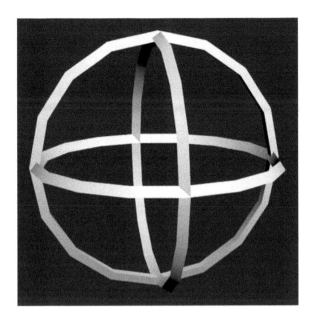

Figure 4.6

Combing *Spline* objects let us create new and exciting controllers that are limited only by your imagination.

Combining Controllers

By combining controllers, we can create even more unique shapes for our rig controls. Just don't obscure the geometry too much, or it will distract the animator too much as well.

```
[SELECT SPLINE CONTROLLER] > RIGHT-CLICK > CONVERT TO: > CONVERT
TO EDITABLE SPLINE
```

```
[SELECT SPLINE CONTROLLER] > MODIFY TAB > GEOMETRY > ATTACH >
[SELECT ANOTHER SPLINE CONTROLLER]
```

4.6.2 On-Screen/On-Viewport Controllers (Animation)

Hang on, I hear you say! Didn't we just go through creating on-screen controllers? Well, no, we didn't! What we created were controllers that live inside the scenes. But what we're going to create here are controllers that fit right over the top of the *viewports* and don't get obscured by what's actually in the scene (Figure 4.7).

These on-screen controllers are really easy to create and use.

Figure 4.7

Sliders can add another level of visual controls to our rigs, but be careful. They sit on top of the screen, so they can get in the way of our assets/rigs if you place them oddly or have too many of them!

On-Screen Controller Creation

Creating on-screen controllers, or *Sliders* as they are commonly known, is very easy. They can be intuitive to use and are easily one of the better ways that we can keep an important control or controls accessible.

CREATE TAB > HELPERS > MANIPULATORS > SLIDER

You probably noticed that there were another two manipulators within the *Slider* creation rollout: the *Cone Angle* and the *Plane Angle*. These things can be used as controllers for our rigs, but a big limitation is not being able to add *Modifiers* to them, and we can't enable their rendering in the viewport or in an actual render, which is sometimes desirable if we want the controllers to be part of a rendered image. It's worth noting these limitations if you'd like to use these controllers in your rigging creations (Figure 4.8).

Once the *Slider* has been placed, you've probably noticed that you can't actually select it—not to edit its position, or even to manipulate its control. Weird, huh? It seems like you have done something wrong, but there is no need to worry. To be able to select the *Slider,* you just have to turn on the option that allows you to select and manipulate it! Do this by clicking the *Select and Manipulate* button on the *Main Toolbar,* which toggles this option on or off (Figure 4.9).

4.6.3 Reaction Controllers (Transform)

At its core, this system allows us to create a master—an object that controls other objects, and for each master, we can have any number of slaves—objects that are controlled by the master. We assign and work with these masters and slaves through the use of the *Reaction Manager* tool and interface.

Although I'm a fan of the *Reaction Manager* and of using *Reaction Controllers* in general, their implementation is a double-edged sword. These kinds of connections can be tedious to create, can take a lot of time, can get confusing, and often require a deeper understanding of how *transform controllers* actually work, and not only that, the learning curve to get good results is steep (Figure 4.10).

Figure 4.8

The *Cone Angle* and *Plane Angle* manipulators might look great, but they have some limitations that need to be acknowledged before using them in a custom rigging solution.

Figure 4.9

In order to use our *Sliders,* we have to enable the *Select and Manipulate* button found on the *Main Toolbar* (see green box). To do this, just click this button.

There are a couple of really good benefits that we inherit by using reaction controllers. The first is that we can manually attach a *Reaction Controller* directly to any track that can have animation data, and the *Reaction Manager* makes creating *Reaction Controllers* and setting their *States* a relatively simple and intuitive process. The second major benefit is that we can actually set multiple states, and doing so allows us to create some interesting and more complex interactions to our rigs. For instance, I've used various states to control the opening and closing of a convertible car's roof, and even transform a robot into a fighter jet. In fact, I like to think about these very complex interactions and multiple states as a way of being able to actually store movement/animation directly into a rig—a very powerful tool that we have at our disposal, I'm sure you'll agree!

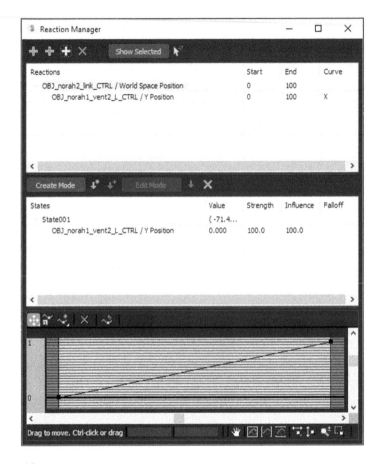

Figure 4.10

The *Reaction Manager* can look daunting at first, but once mastered, it can be an incredibly powerful tool that we can utilize within our rigs.

Creating Reactions Using the *Reaction Manager*

We can use the *Reaction Manager* for creating and modifying *Reaction Controllers*. This window lets you add and delete masters and slaves and define various states for the reactions, and enables us to modify reactions with curves, among other cool stuff.

```
ANIMATION MENU > REACTION MANAGER ...
```

4.6.4 General Controllers (Transform)

As we've already discussed, each and every object that we create in 3ds Max has default *transform controllers* assigned to it. We're able to change these controllers by using *constraints* or even the *Reaction Manager*, but we have many other controllers at our disposal.

The various controllers cause our objects to inherit behaviors and characteristics, sometimes giving us the desired effects and at other times giving us undesirable consequences. The trick with using *transform controllers* is to research, explore, and experiment with the many kinds of controllers that are available.

Controllers such as the *Expression controller, Attachment controller, Noise Position controller, Spring controller,* and *Surface controller* can give really great results if used correctly. I could probably write a whole book on the practical uses of the kinds of controllers available to us, and as such, I really recommend that you spend some time looking though the 3ds Max help guides and tutorials so that you can find out how some of these controllers may benefit you with your rigs.

Assigning Various Position, Rotation and Scale Controllers

Assigning new controllers to objects in 3ds Max is easy. Learning how to use them effectively is the challenging part!

```
[SELECT OBJECT] > MOTION TAB > ASSIGN CONTROLLER > [CHOOSE
CONTROLLER]
```

Or

```
[SELECT OBJECT] > ANIMATION MENU > [CHOOSE FROM THE VARIOUS
CONTROLLERS]
```

If you'd like to combine multiple controllers, be sure to look at the various *list controllers,* as they will help you with this. In fact, this is an advanced but really amazing trick, to be able to have things like a *Position Constraint* affecting an object while we're still able to move it—sneaky, sneaky! We'll actually be using this technique for the upcoming *NORAH* rig.

4.7 Wire Parameters

By wiring together parameters, we are able to link objects so that adjusting one parameter or attribute changes another parameter or attribute directly and automatically—somewhat similar to the *Reaction Manager* and the *Reaction controller.* This enables us to be able to create one- and two-way connections between specified object parameters, meaning that we can even set up custom constraints without actually using *Constraints.* I know, magical CGI voodoo wizardry is afoot!

One-way connections force one parameter to become a slave to the other, and its value changes as the controlling parameter changes, according to a user-defined transfer expression. Think of it like picking up an apple. You become the master, the driving force that directly affects the slave (the apple, in this case). This apple moves and rotates only when you move and rotate it. It's a one-way connection from you to the apple.

For two-way connections, appropriate kinds of parameters are cross-linked so that changing either parameter causes both linked parameters to change at the same time. You can think of these connections as if you are holding hands with someone. If you pull or push, that person is pulled or pushed the same way, and vice versa—a definite two-way connection (Figure 4.11).

Wire Parameters are available only after an object is already selected in the scene, and all object hierarchies should be established before wiring any parameters. If you change the hierarchy of an object that has a *wired parameter*, it will take on new parameters, which could introduce undesired results. I've ruined my own setups many times in the past and had to learn the hard way about the effects of redefining hierarchies after parameters have been wired together. Save yourself the hours of pain, frustration, and trouble by taking note of my failures now. You have been warned!

Wiring Parameters

You need at least one object in your scene so that you can wire one set of parameters to another (yes, you can wire the parameter of an object to another parameter of the same object), either creating a one- or a two-way connection. This tool can be extremely powerful, but remember to only add parameter wiring to an already established hierarchy or else things can go crazy and give undesirable results.

```
[SELECT OBJECT] > RIGHT-CLICK > WIRE PARAMETERS > [CHOOSE
PARAMETER] > [SELECT THE SAME OBJECT OR ANOTHER OBJECT] >
[CHOOSE PARAMETER] > [CHOOSE CONTROL DIRECTION] > CONNECT
```

At the bottom of the *Parameter Wiring* window, there is a section that allows us to use expressions to change the effect of the connection that we are wiring together. This is incredibly useful, and we will definitely be using this in the upcoming chapters. You can experiment with this area right now, of course, and see how your expressions can affect your linked parameters. Please note that although this creates an expression within the wired parameters, it is not an *expression controller,* which can be added in the other way, as described earlier.

4. Common Rigging Techniques

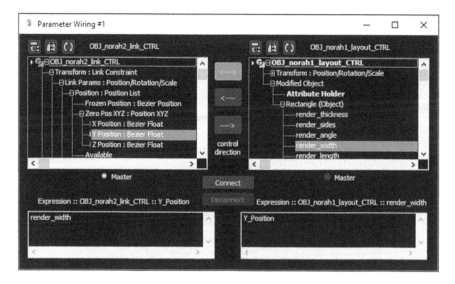

Figure 4.11

Wire Parameters are available on everything you create in the scene. It's worth experimenting with the tool to see what possibilities it offers.

4.8 Custom Attributes

Attributes are used all the time in 3ds Max, and they are extremely useful. By creating a *Sphere* and adjusting its *Radius* attribute, we can already see the benefits of *Attributes* in general, and we can even create our own *custom attributes* to use for our own purposes.

A *custom attribute* is an additional parameter—additional in the sense that it does not directly extend the functionality of the object by default, unlike the *Radius* attribute on the *Sphere*, which does do this. *Custom attributes* affect an object only after *wire parameters, reaction controllers,* or other *transform controllers* are set up to connect the *custom attribute* to another *parameter* in the scene. Experiment with adding *custom attributes* to your objects, and make sure to get used to the built-in *Parameter Types* available and their corresponding *UI Types.*

Creating *custom attributes* is a relatively simple thing to do, and along with the creation of controller objects with which animators can interact, we can enhance the usefulness of these controllers by adding even more functionality and intuitive interactivity. Grab hold of an object in your scene, or create one if you're just trying this out; this is the controller with which we will add the *custom attribute.* Once you're happy with your selection, head on over to the *Modify Tab,* and in the *Modifier List* drop-down menu, add an *Attribute Holder.* The *Attribute*

Holder modifier provides a user interface on the *Modify Panel* to which we can add *custom attributes*. The *Attribute Holder* is an empty modifier with no user interface of its own; the interface consists solely of attributes you assign to it. Right now, we haven't assigned any attributes so this interface is fresh, clean, and completely blank!

With the *Attribute Holder* now sitting at the top of the *Modifier Stack*, we can start adding *custom attributes* by selecting *Parameter Editor (Alt + 1)* from the *Animation Menu*. This *Parameter Editor* pops up in a new floating window that has many options for adding *custom attributes* to our objects, modifiers, materials, and animation tracks (Figure 4.12).

Figure 4.12

With an *Attribute Holder* added to a controller, we can use the *Parameter Editor* to add a number of *custom attributes,* with which we can link to other parameters in our scene.

Adding an *Attribute Holder* and Creating Custom Attributes

The addition of the *Attribute Holder* really cleans up the *Modify Panel* of our objects, and it should be added to all controllers, even if they don't require any custom attributes. However, by adding specific *custom attributes,* we can create dynamic and multifunctional controllers for our animators.

```
[SELECT OBJECT] > MODIFY PANEL > MODIFIER LIST > ATTRIBUTE HOLDER

[SELECT OBJECT] > ANIMATION MENU > PARAMETER EDITOR ... ALT + 1 >
[CREATE AND ADD CUSTOM ATTRIBUTES]
```

There are a number of options within the *Parameter Editor,* and if you're unfamiliar with this tool, it's really worth spending time to experiment and test things out. However, no matter which options you choose or how many *custom attributes* you add to your selected object, they won't do anything until we wire their *parameters,* create *reaction controllers,* or assign another kind of *transform controller,* such as an *expression controller.*

4.9 Modifiers

Modifiers literally modify an object that they are applied to (as you might guess by their name), and each *Modifier* behaves completely different. Due to these great differences, it is impossible to cover what each *Modifier* does, at least in the amount of space I have in these pages. It is important to know how to assign a *Modifier* to an object, and basic knowledge of at least a few of them can really enhance your rigging skills, so it's worth spending some time just experimenting with them.

Adding a *Modifier*

Adding *Modifiers* is incredibly easy and intuitive. Using or knowing how to use *Modifiers* is where the challenge comes in!

```
[SELECT OBJECT] > MODIFY PANEL > MODIFIER LIST > [ANY OPTION]
```

You may have noticed that there are three sections to the *Modifiers* that we have available. There are some notable differences that should be noted with these:

- *Selection Modifiers:*
  - Affect the *subobject selection* of an object.
- *World Space Modifiers (WSMs):*
  - Calculated in world-space.

Figure 4.13

Modifiers come in three different flavors; 1) Selection Modifiers, 2) World-Space Modifiers, 3) Object-Space Modifiers.

- *Object Space Modifiers:*
  - Calculated in object-space (local).

These differences might seem logical and subtle, but they can drastically affect the effect of a *Modifier* that is attached to an object. As a word of caution—be careful with those *WSMs* (Figure 4.13)!

4.10 *Pivots* and Movable *Pivots*

Pivots are created for every object that we create, and we can edit the *Pivot* of an object by going over to the *Hierarchy Panel,* with an object selected, and editing it from there.

Modifying an Object's *Pivot*

Grab an object and head to the *Hierarchy Panel* to get access to various *Pivot* adjustment options.

```
[SELECT OBJECT] > HIERARCHY PANEL > PIVOT BUTTON > ADJUST PIVOT
ROLLOUT
```

There is only one problem with this method—the fact that these *Pivots* allow users to move them, but don't allow us to animate the movement. Now, we can do this by creating a number of objects and using *Wire Parameters* and various *transform controllers,* which works just fine. But an easier way is to use a *transform controller* for the *CAT* rigging system that is built into 3ds Max. The controller that you're looking for is called *CATHDPivotTrans,* and it can be added to any object in your scene. Use the techniques discussed in this chapter to add this controller to an object, and be sure to read about how to use it correctly in the 3ds Max help files.

4.11 Memory Refresh

See Table 4.1.

Table 4.1 **Memory Refresh: Common Rigging Techniques**

CREATING AND EDITING BONES
```
CREATE TAB > SYSTEMS > STANDARD > BONES
Or
ANIMATION MENU > BONE TOOLS ...
```

ADDING INVERSE KINEMATICS TO BONES AND HIERARCHIES
```
[SELECT PARENT IN HIERARCHY] > ANIMATION MENU > IK SOLVERS > HI
SOLVER
```

SKINNING AND THE SKIN DEFORMER
```
[SELECT OBJECT FOR SKINNING] > MODIFY TAB > MODIFIER LIST > OBJECT-
SPACE MODIFIERS > SKIN
Or
[SELECT OBJECT FOR SKINNING] > MODIFIERS MENU > ANIMATION > SKIN
```

ADDING CONSTRAINTS
```
[SELECT OBJECT] > ANIMATION MENU > CONSTRAINTS > [ANY OPTION]
```

CREATING VIEWPORT CONTROLLERS
```
CREATE TAB > SHAPES > SPLINES > [ANY OPTION]
```

(Continued)

Table 4.1 (*Continued*) Memory Refresh: Common Rigging Techniques

ENABLING VIEWPORT RENDERING OF CONTROLLER OBJECTS

```
[SELECT SPLINE CONTROLLER] > MODIFY TAB > RENDERING > ENABLE IN
 VIEWPORT > ON
[SELECT SPLINE CONTROLLER] > MODIFY TAB > RENDERING > SIDES > 3
[SELECT SPLINE CONTROLLER] > MODIFY TAB > INTERPOLATION > STEPS > 3
```

COMBINING CONTROLLERS

```
[SELECT SPLINE CONTROLLER] > RIGHT-CLICK > CONVERT TO: > CONVERT TO
 EDITABLE SPLINE
[SELECT SPLINE CONTROLLER] > MODIFY TAB > GEOMETRY > ATTACH > [SELECT
 ANOTHER SPLINE CONTROLLER]
```

ON-SCREEN CONTROLLER CREATION

```
CREATE TAB > HELPERS > MANIPULATORS > SLIDER
```

CREATING REACTIONS USING THE REACTION MANAGER

```
ANIMATION MENU > REACTION MANAGER ...
```

ASSIGNING VARIOUS POSITION, ROTATION AND SCALE CONTROLLERS

```
[SELECT OBJECT] > MOTION TAB > ASSIGN CONTROLLER > [CHOOSE CONTROLLER]
Or
[SELECT OBJECT] > ANIMATION MENU > [CHOOSE FROM THE VARIOUS
 CONTROLLERS]
```

WIRING PARAMETERS

```
[SELECT OBJECT] > RIGHT-CLICK > WIRE PARAMETERS > [CHOOSE PARAMETER] >
 [SELECT THE SAME OBJECT OR ANOTHER OBJECT] > [CHOOSE PARAMETER] >
 [CHOOSE CONTROL DIRECTION] > CONNECT
```

ADDING AN ATTRIBUTE HOLDER AND CREATING CUSTOM ATTRIBUTES

```
[SELECT OBJECT] > MODIFY PANEL > MODIFIER LIST > ATTRIBUTE HOLDER
 [SELECT OBJECT] > ANIMATION MENU > PARAMETER EDITOR ... ALT + 1 >
 [CREATE AND ADD CUSTOM ATTRIBUTES]
```

ADDING A MODIFIER

```
[SELECT OBJECT] > MODIFY PANEL > MODIFIER LIST > [ANY OPTION]
```

MODIFYING AN OBJECT'S PIVOT

```
[SELECT OBJECT] > HIERARCHY PANEL > PIVOT BUTTON > ADJUST PIVOT ROLLOUT
```

4.12 Summary

There are many other techniques and tools that are commonly used when rigging organic or hard-surfaced geometry in 3ds Max, but for the purposes of this chapter, we have covered the basics of what we need to know to create the *NORAH* rig successfully. It's important to note that these tools and methods are emulated in every other 3D application too. OK—the names of the tools are different, and the processes are also different, but the core foundations and fundamentals are always the same. This means that although the tools here are specific to 3ds Max, once we've learned their uses, we can transfer that information to other 3D applications, and after a short (or not-so-short) learning process on the new software, we should be able to switch relatively easily. It is, after all, core knowledge that is important, not the tools that we use…a bad artist always blames his tools, or so I hear!

I'm hopeful that what we have covered here has been a good refresher for you, but if these methods are new to you, I'd suggest spending some time experimenting with them before moving on. We will cover these with more specific details relating to our actual rig later, but having a good understanding of their operations and restrictions is advised.

Go on. Check them out. I'll wait for you!

…

…

…

Ready? Okay, let's get to the real rigging!

5

Base Rig

Welcome to the main event!

The rigging of our steampunk locomotive, *NORAH,* is where we are going to spend the majority of our time in this book. It is not only the most complex area of discussion, but it also has the most in-depth stages, or phases, of 3 Stage Asset Build (3SAB) that we will be covering.

Although we've just spent some time preparing for rigging and looking at common techniques in the previous chapters, the *Base Rig* forms the first stage of 3SAB as it relates to the rigging process. There is a lot of information to be found here, but fear not, things are broken down and placed into logical, easy-to-follow, and manageable sections, which should make the rigging journey fun, entertaining, and accessible. It's during this phase that we will lay out the core components of the rig so that we have a strong, solid, and very reliable starting point to work from. The other, more complicated stages will take their cues from the *Base Rig* that we're building now, and if that *Base Rig* is not stable, everything else can be broken easily. When complete, this *Base Rig* will make sure that we are ready for further development and create a great starting point for what is going to become an incredibly awesome, but technically complex, mechanical rig that contains features that can be animated as well as automated.

5.1 *ROOT* Node

The *ROOT* node acts as the top node in the hierarchical chain for our rigs, and it is quite literally the root of everything! Often, it is needed by real-time video game engines and crowd simulation tools, but it should really be included in every single rig that you make. This node is not only important for those systems, but it also allows us to keep our rigging hierarchies clean and contained under this one *ROOT*.

Additionally, it allows us to use this node to store information and *Custom Attributes* and to have a defined point of reference that is helpful for building tools, scripts, and plug-ins. It's also pretty helpful if this rigged asset is moving through a real production pipeline. As you can tell, it's a pretty important piece of the rigging puzzle.

Creating a *ROOT* node is as easy as creating any object and placing it at the center of the world, *XYZ[0,0,0]*, and then parenting everything else under it. Personally, I prefer to use an *ExposeTM* helper object for my *ROOT* nodes, as they include a number of special attributes. So, cool stuff for free—how could anyone say no?! Oh, I should mention that if you do decide to use an *ExposeTM* helper, some real-time game engines don't know what to do with it—I'm looking at you, Unity3D! But, no worries—rig it like this for now, but if you're sending it to an engine, you should probably switch out this node for a *Dummy* or *Point Helper* because those things work just fine.

Creating a *ROOT* Node

The *ROOT* node is going to form the upper-most element/object of your rig, where everything else will be linked/parented to. It's easy to create, keeps things clean and organized, and helps with transformation issues. So, it's worthwhile to put it in.

```
CREATE TAB > HELPERS > STANDARD > EXPOSETM

MOVE TO XYZ[0,0,0]

RENAME TO "OBJ_norah_ROOT"
```

Use the *Select and Link* tool to parent *OBJ_norah_GEO_GRP* under the newly created *ROOT* node, and we're all done with this part. I'd suggest saving at this point!

5.2 Controller Group, Rigging Group, and Work-in-Progress (WIP) Group

The next thing on the agenda is to create a group that will eventually hold all the in-viewport or on-viewport controllers that we will be creating for our animators to manipulate. This is very simple and requires us to create a *Point*

Helper positioned at the center of the scene, *XYZ[0,0,0]*. Then we can parent this node to the *ROOT* node and rename it as *OBJ_norah_CTRL_GRP*.

Next, we repeat the exact same steps for the rigging and the Work-in-Progress (WIP) groups, and they are named *OBJ_norah_RIG_GRP* and *WIP*, respectively (Figure 5.1).

We'll actually be using *Point Helpers* for most of the rigging elements for the locomotive. So get friendly—we're going to be spending a lot of time together!

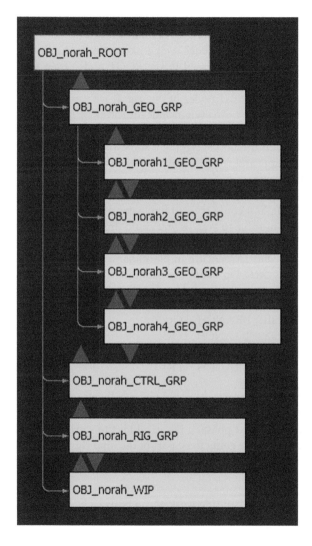

Figure 5.1

The basic hierarchy of this rig is now in place, sitting under the *ROOT* node.

5.3 *BRANCH* Nodes

If we were creating an organic rig, we would go ahead and start placing a node, whether that be a *Point Helper,* a *Dummy,* or a *Bone,* at the *Center Of Gravity (COG)* location. However, this is a steampunk locomotive, a machine that is mechanical and metallic—full of hard-surface geometry. Sure, it has a *COG,* but that is irrelevant for our rigging purposes. Instead, our focus shifts to where the main base of control will be for each carriage. This primary location of control can be represented by a *BRANCH* node instead of the *COG* node. Once again, *BRANCH* nodes are our best rigging friends—*Point Helpers*—and we are going to create one for each of the carriages (a total of four).

Why the name *BRANCH* node? Well, I like to think of it like a tree. You have the tree roots...yeah, you guessed it, the *ROOT* node. Then you have the tree trunk, those core groups that we just created. Then the trunk has branches, which of course are the *BRANCH* nodes of our rig. If we want, or have to, get really complex with our rigs, we can even include the leaves, or *LEAF* nodes—something that we won't actually do for the *NORAH* rig, as it's not really needed. I'm sure that you can tell that this method of rigging is somewhat abstract, but it simplifies the thinking about large and complicated rigs, and I hope that you can see the value of thinking this way.

Anyway, enough theory—the location of these *BRANCH* nodes are entirely at your discretion. You could try and find a good place to start the branch from, a spot that feels intuitive to you, or you could drop them all at the center of the scene, *XYZ[0,0,0].* I'll leave that choice up to you.

Once all the *Point Helpers* are in place, name them and parent them under *OBJ_norah_RIG_GRP.* I'm using the usual naming conventions and adding a number next to the name so that each carriage is denoted specifically (Figure 5.2):

- OBJ_norah1_BRANCH_LOC
- OBJ_norah2_BRANCH_LOC
- OBJ_norah3_BRANCH_LOC
- OBJ_norah4_BRANCH_LOC

With everything in place, we could technically attach the geometry to these *BRANCH* nodes and call it quits for the *Base Rig.* However, to make things easier as we move into the next phase, it is a good idea to start breaking down each of the components that are going to be part of the final rig.

5.4 Component Breakdown

We have some time-consuming work ahead of us right now. *NORAH* has many different elements, and they all need special attention at every stage of this rig's development. For this stage, the *Base Rig,* we need to use *Point Helpers* once again (or something similar if you prefer) to break each component into separate sections. With each component in its own section, we can then attach the

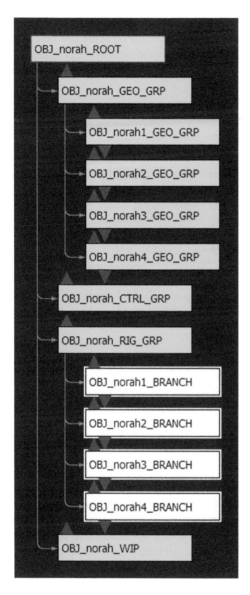

Figure 5.2

The *BRANCH* nodes are now in place.

geometry elements so that manipulation of the *Point Helpers* actually affects the model. This is a little different from organic rigs, in which we would usually add *Bones/Joints* and use the *Point Helpers* more as just a layout/blueprint. Although they could technically be used in the place of *Bones/Joints* as well, it's just a matter of how you like to rig.

As we will be using a lot of *Point Helpers*, we need to align them to various parts of the model. However, as we've already reset the geometry pivots to the center of the scene (*XYZ[0,0,0]*), we have to use the *Align* tool with a method that does not reference the *Pivot* of the geometry. It's a little inconvenient, but it doesn't really affect us too much.

Aligning Objects

As we reset the *Pivots* of our objects to the center of the scene, we can't use them to align the objects. Luckily, the *Align* tool allows us to choose a number of options to align to. We should be able to use the *Pivot* of the *Point Helper* to align to the center of each wheel, but try the various options and see which works best.

[SELECT OBJECT] > MAIN TOOLBAR > ALIGN

Be prepared—this is not particularly challenging, but because it takes so long, it requires a lot of patience and dedication to complete successfully. Here we go!

5.4.1 *NORAH* No. 1: Branch

The first carriage of this model is by far the most complex section, so it requires the most work as we go through each of the phases. I suggest that the first thing to do is to hide everything else in the scene that doesn't correspond to this first section. This is going to make things a lot easier. As we already have the *BRANCH* node in place, we can jump straight into any element that we want to work with, as the order in which we tackle things at this stage doesn't really matter (Figure 5.3).

5.4.1.1 *The Bell*

We'll start things off really easily by working on the bell found at the very front of the train. It requires three *Point Helpers*—the first at the base of the bell, the second for the bell itself, and the last for the clapper found inside. The bell and clapper *Point Helpers* need to be positioned so that their *Pivot* points can control the bell as would be expected, and the base *Point Helper* just needs to be placed at the base of the bell. I'll not go into specifics here, as the setup is very easy.

When you're happy with the locations of these elements, remember to name them all correctly, parent them together, and then back up to the *BRANCH* node, as shown in Figure 5.4.

5.4.1.2 *The Bumper*

The bumper is another simple element, and we need at least three *Point Helpers* to create it. The first is for the base, and the other two are for the ends of the bumper bars. If you want, you could add another two *Point Helpers*, which would be placed at the beginning of each bumper bar, but this is completely optional.

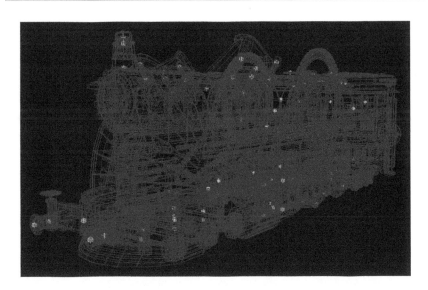

Figure 5.3

The completed first carriage component layout with all *Point Helpers* in place.

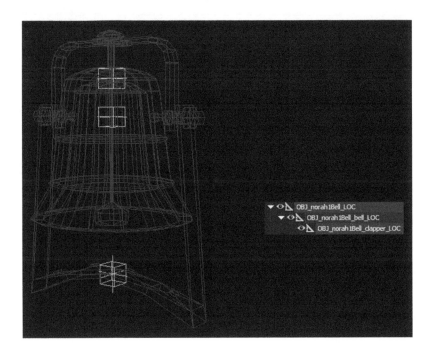

Figure 5.4

The bell setup is fast and simple.

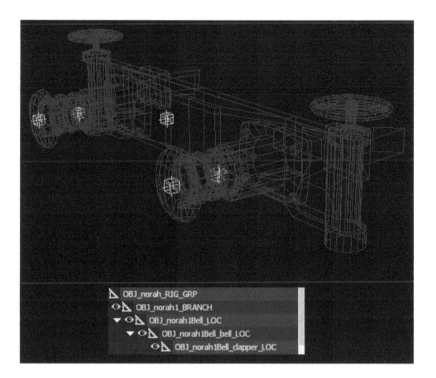

Figure 5.5

The bumper setup is just as simple as the bell component.

Once everything is in place, just name things correctly and put them into the *BRANCH* node hierarchy (Figure 5.5).

5.4.1.3 The Joiner

Now, at the rear of the first carriage, one or two *Point Helpers* can be used to create the joiner. So long as you have at least one of these positioned so that the pivot is at the rotation point of the joiner's arm, all will be good! Name and parent the elements to finish up, as always (Figure 5.6).

5.4.1.4 The Valves

At the top of the first carriage is a number of valves. If we want these to be able to be rotated, we can just create a helper for each of them—it's very easy (Figure 5.7). As with every section, rename and parent them—I'll stop mentioning this now, as I know you get the idea (but just remember that you have to do this for every element).

5.4.1.5 Front and Rear Budges

The front and rear budges contain three wheels apiece, each with suspension. Additionally, each budge has a suspension. We have the opportunity to add a

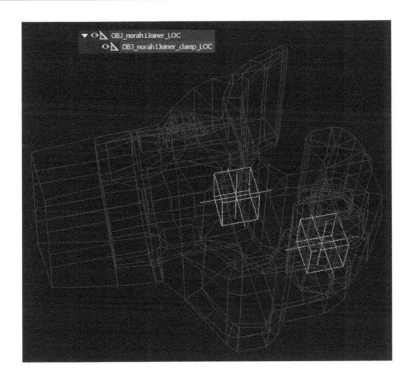

Figure 5.6

Remember that the pivot position needs to be placed correctly in order for the joiner to work properly.

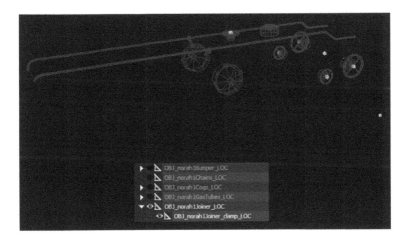

Figure 5.7

No big deal here—these valves just need a *Point Helper* added so that they can be rotated.

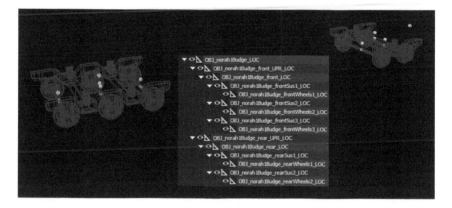

Figure 5.8

The front and rear budges contain wheels and suspension.

number of *Point Helpers* for the budge, wheels, and each of the suspensions. It won't actually be necessary for the setup that we need because getting this close to the wheels is not going to happen, but I've included them just in case you feel adventurous (Figure 5.8).

5.4.1.6 The Cogs

Technically, the cogs are driven by the engine, and as they are exactly the same on either side of the train, we only have to focus on one side. However, if we were to anticipate that this model will be involved in a crash or some other kind of commotion that requires the cogs to be driven separately, we would have to rig both sides.

For the requirements of this book, the locomotive will not need anything more than a simple setup that is driven from the engine—even though an engine doesn't really exist on the model! So, with that said, I'm going to create *Point Helpers* in the center of the train. These *Point Helpers* will affect both sides of the train, but this means that we have to rig only one time for each cog, cutting our time in half—nice! (See Figure 5.9.)

5.4.1.7 Chains

We will treat the chains just like the cogs and simply place one *Point Helper* in the center of the train, between the chains on either side. Don't worry about anything else right now—we'll work out the complexities and specifics of rigging chains later in Chapter 6 (Figure 5.10).

5.4.1.8 Pistons

Each piston needs three *Point Helpers* positioned at the piston head, the rotating bar, and the pivot section in the middle. I'm sure those things have very specific names, but I'm no engineer!

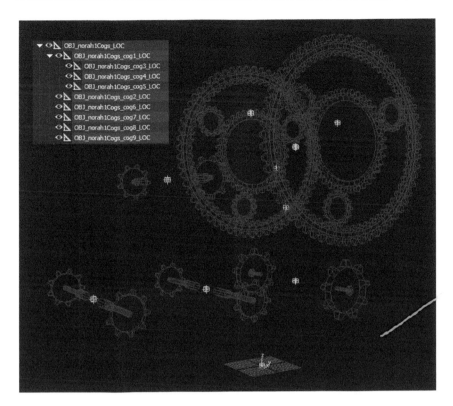

Figure 5.9

Each cog requires one *Point Helper* placed at the center between the left and right cogs. This will allow us to rig just one *Point Helper* that will affect two cogs at the same time.

We also need another *Point Helper* to allow the main rotation, positioned in the center of the main bar and at the center of the train to use as the base for the rest of them. I've created *Point Helpers* for both sides this time, so each piston has its own setup.

The parenting and naming of all these *Point Helpers* can be a little bit confusing, so just take your time and follow Figure 5.11 for clarity.

5.4.1.9 Wheels and Beams

Between the front and rear budges, we have the main wheels, which are moved directly from the engine via the cogs and chains. The wheels require a *Point Helper* to be placed in the center of them, and each of the beams requires a *Point Helper* placed at the start and end of it. These beams are directly driven by the wheels so they can be linked to the directly (Figure 5.12).

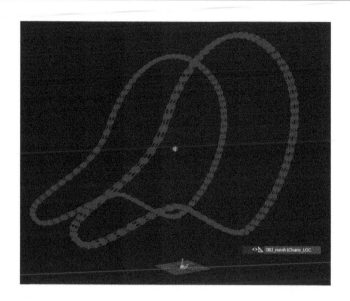

Figure 5.10

The chains just require a single *Point Helper* for now.

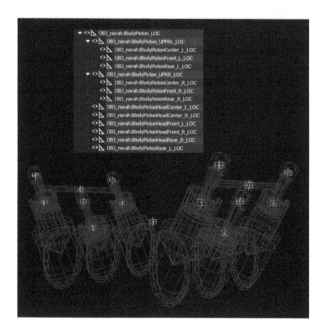

Figure 5.11

A number of *Point Helpers* are needed for the pistons, and they are placed specifically so that the correct movements can be created during the next rigging phase.

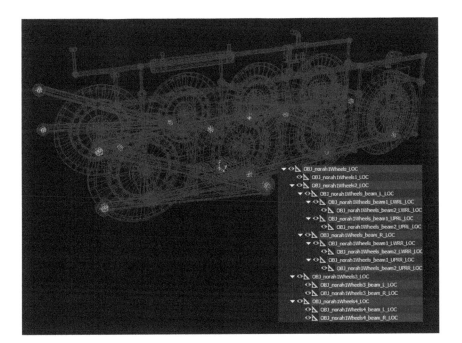

Figure 5.12

The wheels and beams need to be placed in a specific hierarchy in order to work correctly.

5.4.1.10 Side Pistons

The side pistons are controlled by the beams coming from the wheels, but we'll make that connection in the upcoming rigging phases. For now, each side piston requires *Point Helper* placed at the beginning and end of the suspensions (Figure 5.13).

5.4.1.11 First Carriage Tubes/Hoses

The final thing that we need to worry about is the openings for the tubes that come from the fuel system on the second carriage. We only need to find these areas and place a *Point Helper* at each of these openings. This is going to dictate where those tubes get snapped when all the pieces of the entire carriage are set up to work together (Figure 5.14).

5.4.2 *NORAH* No. 2: Branch

The second carriage is coincidentally the second most complex carriage to rig. Luckily, it is much easier than the first, but we will be following the same kind of procedure. So, get prepared for more *Point Helper* creation (Figure 5.15).

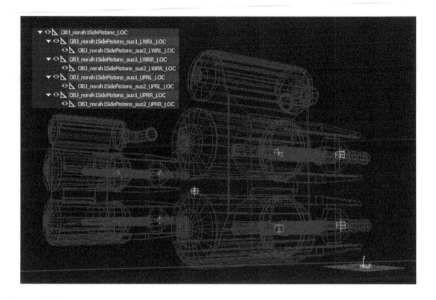

Figure 5.13

For now, the side pistons just need a quick setup.

5.4.2.1 Bogie, Wheels, and Joiners

The bogie, or the lower section of this carriage, is pretty solid, so the setup isn't too difficult but it does require some effort to setup correctly. There are 10 mini-wheels on this, which all have to rotate, so each requires its own *Point Helper* (Figure 5.16).

Because this part of the train is one of the middle carriages, there is a joiner on both the front and rear sections. This is exactly the same setup that we did on the first carriage, so I won't repeat things here.

5.4.2.2 Chains and Suspension

We only need a locator (*Point Helper*) placed at the connecting areas of the chains and suspension. You will find four suspension rods going into the bogie and two chains at the front and back of the tender—that big ball thing!

5.4.2.3 Tender and Fans

With the lower section (the bogie) out of the way, we can quickly move on to the upper section (tender). The tender is split into two sections, the upper and lower, split by the large central fan.

On the lower section, we need to add locators for the four suspension rods and the two chains. Then we can add a locator in the center of that big fan (Figure 5.17).

On the top, we have another two fans, but they are a lot smaller. Add a locator for each of these.

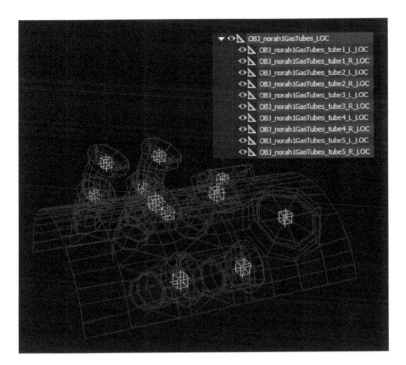

Figure 5.14

Each of the fuel tube entrances on the first carriage needs a *Point Helper* in order for us to dictate where those tubes will actually be attached.

5.4.2.4 Second Carriage Tubes/Hoses

We need a locator for each of the tubes/hoses that comes out of the upper part of the tender. This procedure is pretty basic, and just requires the use of a *Point Helper* at the start of the tube/hose and a *Point Helper* at the end. Repeat for each one of the tubes/hoses!

5.4.3 *NORAH* No. 3: Branch

Carriage number three is even easier than carriage two…I know, how easy could we possibly make this, right? Well, just wait for carriage number four!

Anyway, this carriage carries a bomb—for reasons that we will never know. Now, we will get in there and set up the bomb itself, but you'll probably notice a number of wires twisted and wrapped around the frame of this carriage. We could get in there and rig every single element of these wires, and if we were working on a production where we see a close-up of this section, we would need to do that. However, for our needs, it's really overkill, and it can be done using various deformers. So, for the purposes of clarity and in order to focus on other areas of the model, these additional wires will be forgotten about. Don't worry—things will still look awesome (Figure 5.18).

Figure 5.15

The completed component layout of the second carriage.

5.4.3.1 Frame and Joiners

The frame itself is rock-solid…actually, it's probably more reinforced-steel solid. So, that's an easy setup for us, as it requires just one locator.

This is another one of those central carriages, so we have a joiner at both the front and back. And, yeah, you guessed it—these both need a locator in order for us to be able to rotate the hinge at some point in the future.

5.4.3.2 Front and Rear Budges

The front and rear budges of this section are exactly the same as those found on the first carriage of our *NORAH* model. That means we have the budge, suspensions, and wheels to set up. Just copy what we did for the first carriage and we are good.

5.4.3.3 Bomb

The bomb itself requires a locator in the center. From there, we have a number of chains that hold it in place and suspend it from the frame. For now, just as we did for the second carriage, we need to add locators to the start and end of each chain (Figure 5.19).

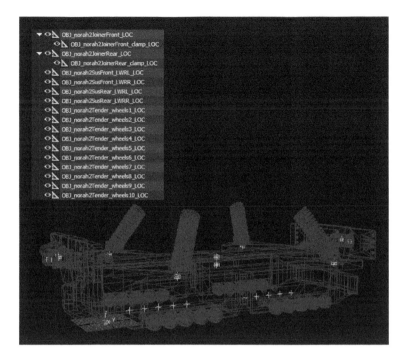

Figure 5.16

There are lots of mini-wheels on this carriage. Fun!

5.4.4 *NORAH* No. 4: Branch

You guessed it—the fourth and final carriage is by far the easiest. We have no new components in here, just a large mass of the main carriage, budges at the front and rear, and joiners. We'll be duplicating the exact same setups that we've already completed in previous sections, so this shouldn't take long at all (Figure 5.20).

5.4.4.1 *Front/Rear Budges and Joiners*

There's not much I need to explain here. The budges are the same found on other carriages, as are the joiners, so just duplicate those setups and add them. Oh, and the reason that this carriage has a joiner at the back is that we may need to have other carriages attached there at some point. We're just keeping our options open!

5.5 Attaching the Geometry

Right now, if we try to transform (move, rotate, or scale) any of the *BRANCH* nodes or any of the locators (*Point Helpers*), we don't have any effect over the geometry of the locomotive—not exactly the desired result that we want. So we need to get those locators affecting the model somehow.

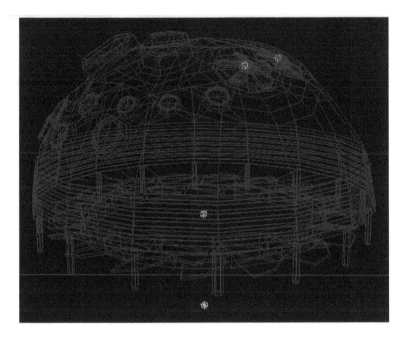

Figure 5.17

The tender has two sections, divided by the large fan in the center.

The most obvious way in which we could influence the geometry is to use the *Select and Link* tool to parent the geometry under the corresponding locators. You know what? This is a perfectly feasible way of doing that, but there are many other ways to achieve the result, and this method would go against that principle of clean hierarchies, which would go against my beliefs. In fact, due to the number of locators that we have already added, things wouldn't work out exactly like we want them to anyway.

So, instead of parenting the geometry under the various locators, we have five other options available to us:

- *Constraints*
- *Wire Parameters*
- *Reaction Controllers*
- *Expressions*
- *Skinning*

The thing is, only *Skinning* is going to give us the desired results that we need. Sure, *Constraints* would probably work out just fine too, but *Skinning* is so much more adaptable—even for hard-surface models. Remember that *Skin* can be deformed by any object in Autodesk 3ds Max—it doesn't have to be *Bones*.

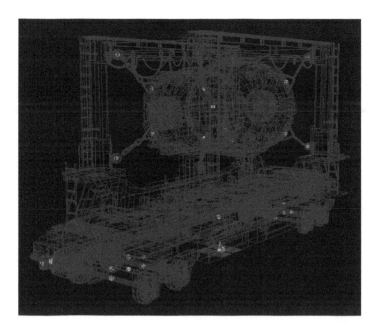

Figure 5.18

The completed component layout of the third carriage.

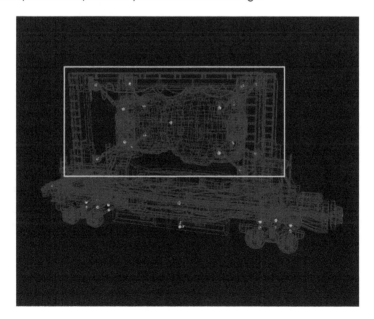

Figure 5.19

The locators (*Point Helpers*) from the third carriage, all set and ready for rigging.

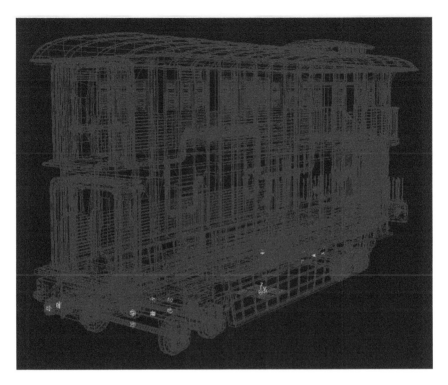

Figure 5.20

The completed component layout of the fourth carriage.

By adding a *Skin Modifier* to our geometry, we can influence specific areas of our model by using vertices to decide what sections move with the specific locators. This is going to take some time to do, so add *Skin* to your model, choose the correct *Point Helpers* in which to affect it, change the deformations by using the *Vertices* and generally keep all *Skin Weights* set to either *1* or *0;* this will ensure that the geometry is kept visibly solid. You may notice one or two areas that need additional things to deform correctly, I'm thinking springs and chains here, but don't worry about that, just for now. Get things looking as good as possible, and we'll address the geometry that needs additional deformers in the next phase.

5.6 Adding the Controllers

Working on creating all of those *Point Helpers* is a slow and tedious task, but it was a necessary evil that will make things a lot easier as we venture into the next phase of rigging. To celebrate the completion of that dull section, I think that this

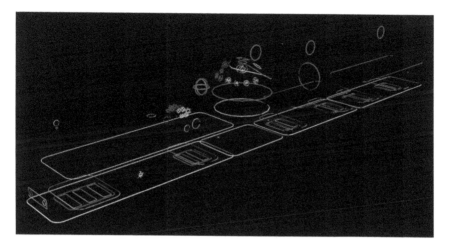

Figure 5.21

Controllers are created and ready for rigging. Colors have been set to Color Coding from Chapter 1.

is a good time to create some preliminary controllers for our rig. I'm going to be using *Splines* to create my controllers, and because a lot of controls are needed, I'll be keeping the shapes of these controllers as simple as I can.

It's important to note that each of these controllers needs to have its *pivot points* match and line up exactly with its corresponding *Point Helpers* in the scene. If we don't do this, not only will the pivots be off, but manipulating the controllers won't give us the results that we desire (Figure 5.21).

With the controllers in place and named correctly, we need to grab all of them and make sure that they are sitting under the *OBJ_norah_CTRL_GRP* node. We'll be attaching them during the *Animation/Automation Rigging* phase.

5.7 Memory Refresh

See Table 5.1.

Table 5.1 Memory Refresh: Base Rig

CREATING A ROOT NODE

```
CREATE TAB > HELPERS > STANDARD > EXPOSETM
MOVE TO XYZ[0,0,0]
RENAME TO "OBJ_norah_ROOT"
```

ALIGNING OBJECTS

```
[SELECT OBJECT] > MAIN TOOLBAR > ALIGN
```

5.8 Summary

This *Base Rig* has been a lot of work—simple, boring and tedious, using many *Point Helpers,* renaming elements, and setting up hierarchies. But now that this is all set up, we can confidently jump into the *Animation/Automation Rig* confidently. We have all the locators we need in place, we have the geometry affected by those locators, and we even have most of the controllers in the scene, raring to go. All we need to do now is connect everything together…easier said than done, but let's get to it!

6

Animation and Automation Rig

Part 1

Driven by the *Base Rig*, the *Animation and Automation Rig* contains all the controls and complicated interactive elements of the rig. This stage forms the interface for animators to influence the models directly, allowing them to breathe life into these static objects. Additionally, this is the phase of rigging production where we can predefine and automate movements that are either specific, technical, or complex, and/or would just be overly tedious to animate manually. In comparison to the *Base Rig*, this stage requires a lot more technical input from us, and the tasks that we need to run through can be challenging. It is for those reasons that we will spend a good amount of time in this section.

One thing that is great about working on an asset such as *NORAH* is that we can start rigging pretty much any section that first piques our interest. Of course, with sections that are driven by other sections or are linked in some way, it makes sense to start with the section or element that starts the chain reaction. But for the most part, there is no real set order for us to do things in. So feel free to jump around and rig in whichever order you'd like. I've grouped things together so that if you start a section, you will complete all the elements related to that area. Once that component is complete, you can jump to something else, as they won't affect one another! As I'm writing this, I will be working through things systematically, starting with the first carriage in this chapter and the second, third, and fourth carriages in the next chapter. This is due to both the complexity and the sheer volume of things that need to be done in order to get the rig for this train to work correctly.

There's a lot going on in this section, and it's important to realize that were we to animate all of the train's intricacies, it would be time consuming, difficult, and mind-numbingly boring! It's our job not to let this happen.

6.1 *NORAH*: Carriage No. 1

No matter what we do, this rig is going to be a challenge. As a whole, the rig itself seems like an unwieldy, complex monstrosity that is going to explode our brains! Well, it might be just me, but there is certainly a lot going on in this rig, and it makes sense to break any huge task into smaller tasks that we can combine, kind of like what we did with the *Base Rig*. This removes at least the perception of unbearable complexity into smaller, more manageable parts. Again, the most logical breakdown is to focus our attention on each carriage. From there, we can break them down even further, into each and every element and component that creates the carriage itself.

As already mentioned, the first carriage is by far the most complex, technical, and time-consuming (Figure 6.1). It is also the one carriage that affects all the other carriages, as this is not only what everything is linked to, but it also contains the driving force behind the locomotive, the engine. Of course, there is not really an engine sitting inside the model, but we do have cogs, chains, pistons, and beams to simulate the appearance of one.

Before we jump into the components, we need to make sure that the *OBJ_norah1_layout_CTRL* works as expected. Make sure that the pivot point of the controller matches up with the *OBJ_norah1_BRANCH* locator in both *position* and *orientation*. From there, we can use the *Link Constraint* to link the locator to the controller.

Creating a *Link Constraint*

A *Link Constraint* works just like parenting in a hierarchy—but without actually needing to create a hierarchy! It's incredibly helpful, but you have to watch out for double-transformations and dependency loops between objects.

[SELECT OBJECT] > ANIMATION MENU > CONSTRAINTS > LINK CONSTRAINT

6.1.1 The Bell

The bell is a very simple setup, as the controllers that we have created directly control the locators. First, we need to sort out the hierarchy of the controllers by

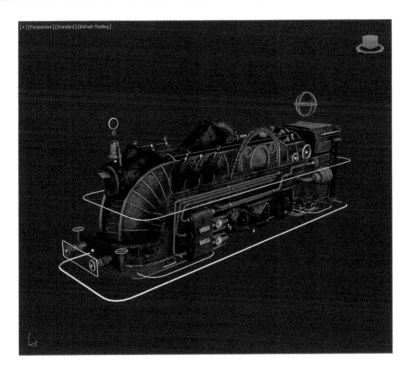

Figure 6.1

The *NORAH*—Carriage No. 1 element breakdown for rigging.

parenting the *OBJ_norah1_clapper_CTRL* to the *OBJ_norah1_bell_CTRL*. Then parent the *OBJ_norah1_bell_CTRL* to the *OBJ_norah1_layout_CTRL*.

This will make sure that the controllers work correctly, but we still need to get those controllers to affect the locators, and in turn the geometry. This is a simple case of just using the *Link Constraint* once again, to make sure that the controllers have an effect on those *Point Helpers* that we created during the *Base Rig*. You should have the bell and clapper set to a *skin weight* of *1* to their respective *Point Helpers*, so if things aren't working out as you expect, this might be the issue!

6.1.2 The Bumper

We could give these bumpers a complex setup if we wanted to, and springs in particular can be handled in a variety of different ways. However, for what we actually need this bumper section to do, there is no need to make things difficult for ourselves. Let's start by getting the controllers into their correct hierarchies first. *OBJ_norah1_bumper_L_CTRL* and the *OBJ_norah1_bumper_R_CTRL* need to be linked to *OBJ_norah1_bumper_CTRL*, which in turn is linked to the *OBJ_norah1_layout_CTRL*. That will make the controllers behave as we expect them to.

OK, so use that *Link Constraint* to attach the relevant locator to the *L* and *R* bumper controls. We haven't spent any time looking at the springs of this section, so things might not be visually working out just yet. Let's take some time to fix that right now.

Obviously, the end points of the bumpers should move along with our controls, while the main section stays rigid. This is easy enough to work out using either *0* or *1* on the *vertex skin weights*. We'll then use carefully placed *Skin Weights* to create the illusion that we have the springs of the bumpers set correctly. We do this by blending the *Skin Weights* from *1* at the end of the bumper to something around *0.1* at the beginning. This creates the illusion that the spring is compressing and stretching as the controllers are moved. The actual movement in the front bumper is small, so this technique works perfectly, and it is relatively painless to set this up correctly (Figure 6.2).

6.1.3 The Joiner

The joiner should open and close with a simple rotation of the controller, so parent that *OBJ_norah1_joinerRear_CTRL* to the *OBJ_norah1_layout_CTRL* and make sure that the *pivot* is in the exact same location as the *Point Helper* that really moves the joiner's geometry. From there, use that *Link Constraint* again so the controller really does control that joiner.

6.1.4 The Valves

We have a total of five valves on the upper section of the first carriage. These controllers all need to be parented into the *OBJ_norah1_layout_CTRL* and a *Link Constraint* needs to be added to their locators. Easy!

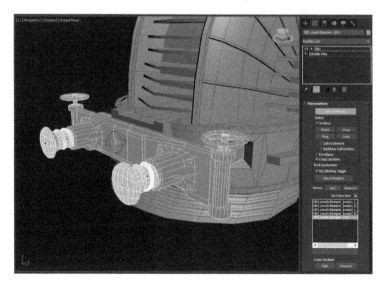

Figure 6.2

The springs on each side of the bumper are replicated by some carefully placed *skin weighting*.

6.1.5 Front and Rear Budges

Both the front and the rear budges include the same kind of setup. Because of this, we will focus on the front for now and repeat the same steps on the rear afterward. Each budge has three controllers and should be parented into a hierarchy as follows:

- OBJ_norah1_layout_CTRL
  - OBJ_norah1_budgeFront_CTRL
    - OBJ_norah1_budgewheelsFront_CTRL
      - OBJ_norah1_budgewheelsFront_1_CTRL
      - OBJ_norah1_budgewheelsFront_2_CTRL
      - OBJ_norah1_budgewheelsFront_3_CTRL

With the hierarchy in place, we once again use the *Link Constraint* to make sure that the correct sections of the model move along with the controllers. Once everything is working correctly, you will no doubt notice that the budge has a number of springs that act as the suspension. If you remember, during the *Base Rig* (section 5.4.1.5), we added some additional *Point Helpers* to cope with these elements. It's at this point that we can go ahead and start to adjust the *skin weights* to simulate the compression of the springs as the controllers are manipulated. However, it's worth taking a moment to think about whether this is really going to be seen. If we are not planning on showing this suspension very close to the camera, the audience wouldn't be able to tell if they are rigged up to move or not. If we don't need it, we can save ourselves a lot of time here!

One thing that we are missing is the rotation of the wheels. We're going to leave this as it is just for now, as they will be controlled via a kind of chain reaction from the main controller, which drives the rotation of the cogs, chains, beams, and wheels (Figure 6.3).

Figure 6.3

The completed setup for the front budge.

With the front budge set up and ready to go, duplicate this exact same setup for the rear budge. Once that's complete, we can move on.

6.1.6 The Engine

Although *NORAH* technically doesn't have an engine inside it, we create the illusion of it having a big, powerful engine, as there are areas that are partly exposed. Of course, this means that we have to do something with those parts that can be seen, and they form the more complicated areas in which we have to rig.

There is a great deal of movement happening in the sections related to the engine, and this continuous, mechanical motion would be tedious to animate manually. Therefore, we have to develop an elegant solution for all these moving parts that gives the animator control without becoming a nightmare to work with.

Seven components go into making this engine section (Figure 6.4):

- Cogs
- Chains
- Pistons
- Wheels
- Beams
- Side pistons
- Budge wheels

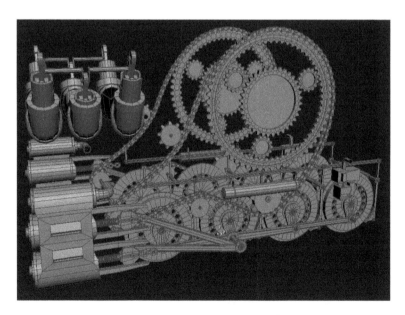

Figure 6.4

Shown here are the seven separate components that create the illusion that this locomotive has an engine.

We need to go through these step by step, as everything links together in a chain reaction spreading from those cogs. The following components need to be driven accurately and automatically from a single input—the one controller that we're going to give to our animator.

6.1.6.1 Cogs

The cogs in this first carriage are what actually drive all the automated elements of this model. The animator controls all this automation by taking hold of the spherical controller *OBJ_norah1_drive_CTRL*. We can quickly use the *Select and Link* tool to make sure that that controller is sitting under the layout controller for this first carriage, and then it will move along with everything correctly.

OK—so we now have a total of 18 cogs on this model, 9 of them on either side of the train. As we have *Point Helpers* already sitting in the center of the train, we are only going to be rigging these 9 locators, and they will affect both sides (this is going to cut down our rigging time in this section). We already should have each cog controlled by a separate *Point Helper*, but it is worth double-checking at this point to see if the *skin weighting* has been set up correctly.

With the *skinning* worked out, let's drop those locators into a hierarchical structure that makes the most sense. Using Figure 6.5 as a reference for the cog numbering, make sure that your hierarchy is exactly the same as this:

- OBJ_norah1Cogs_LOC
  - OBJ_norah1Cogs_cog1_LOC
  - OBJ_norah1Cogs_cogOffset_LOC
    - OBJ_norah1Cogs_cog3_LOC
    - OBJ_norah1Cogs_cog4_LOC
    - OBJ_norah1Cogs_cog5_LOC
  - OBJ_norah1Cogs_cog2_LOC
  - OBJ_norah1Cogs_cog6_LOC
  - OBJ_norah1Cogs_cog7_LOC
  - OBJ_norah1Cogs_cog8_LOC
  - OBJ_norah1Cogs_cog9_LOC

This hierarchy is going to make sure that we can drive the locators correctly from just a single controller. The great thing about this setup is that we're going to be using just *Wire Parameters* and a small mathematical expression to make sure that everything is rotating as it should. Let's jump in and get that first cog (*OBJ_norah1Cogs_cog1_LOC*) rotating.

Start by right-clicking *OBJ_norah1_drive_CTRL* and selecting *Wire Parameters…*from the *Quad Menu* and choose the *Rotate X* parameter. We need to plug that into the *Rotate X* of the locator, so make that connection.

This is going to be a *One-Way Connection*, so don't hesitate to click that button and click *Connect*. We don't need to worry about adding anything mathematical to this connection, so close things down and check that the rotation of the controller

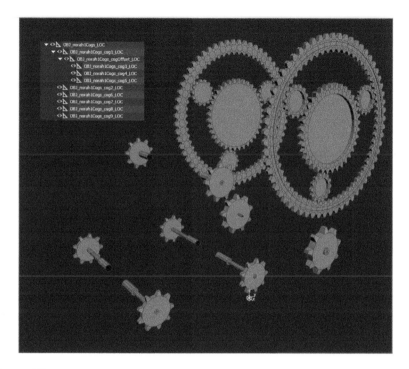

Figure 6.5

There are a total of 18 cogs—9 on either side—which control the chains and wheel rotations of *NORAH*.

affects the cog. Don't worry about those three small cogs spinning with the central cog; we're going to fix that up in just a moment.

For now, wire up the rotation of the *OBJ_norah1Cogs_cog1_LOC* to the *OBJ_norah1Cogs_cogOffset_LOC* using the following expression:

$$-X\_Rotation*2$$

What we've created here is a connection that drives the rotation negatively—in the opposite direction. Then we have increased that rate of rotation by 2. It's a simple way in which to get these cogs to react to one another (Figure 6.6).

Once again, we're going to use the rotation of that first cog to control the rotation of our smaller cogs. There is no real difference to any of the cogs from this point on; we are just creating connections with the *Wire Parameters* tool and adding an expression. Generally, to get the cogs rotating at the correct speeds, we need to use some basic mathematics, which looks like this:

$$Cog*LargeRadius/SmallRadius$$

6. Animation and Automation Rig: Part 1

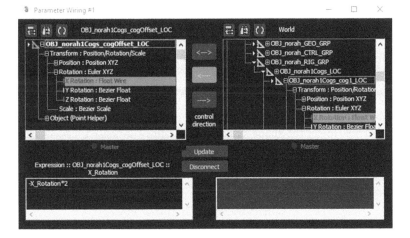

Figure 6.6

OBJ_norah1Cogs_cogOffset_LOC needs to be wired with an expression in order for it to turn in the opposite direction and at the correct rate of rotation.

By using this expression, you should be able to solve rotations in any kind of setup where one object has to rotate around another. Of course, you may need to add a negative value to get the object spinning in the opposite direction, but that's no big deal!

With all that said, use the *Wire Parameters* tool to wire the *Rotate X* from the first cog to the *Rotate X* of one of the smaller cogs. With a connection in place, add the expression:

$$-X\_Rotation*5.143$$

We can now do the same for the other smaller cogs and then create similar connections for the other cogs left in this setup. It can become a little confusing when trying to fit everything together, but stick at it and eventually the repetition will help you make sense of it all.

6.1.6.2 Chains

Those chains need to wrap around the cogs and actually move along with each of the gears as they rotate. There are a number of ways to do this, and for the purposes of this rig, I've opted to use a solution that is relatively fast to set up and looks incredible, but is not 100% accurate.

You may be wondering why I wouldn't choose the most accurate solution for this, but it would honestly be overkill for what we need. If the *NORAH* rig were a product demonstration that needed to be accurate as it was scrutinized, I would choose the most accurate option. However, as this is not a real model, nor are we going to get close enough to see the tiniest nuances, it's just not worth the time to go over a great-looking, not-perfect rig for absolute accuracy. Maybe we could cover the more accurate version in the next chapter, but who knows what will happen? (Don't jump ahead or look at the contents page, or else you won't be surprised!)

All right—the first thing that we need to do is to create a *Spline* that follows the shape of the chain that is currently modeled. It's easy enough to do with the *Line* tool, which is found under the *Shapes Menu* in the *Create Tab*. Make sure to set the *Initial Type* to *Smooth* and keep the *Drag Type* to *Bezier,* which will make our *Line* object as smooth as possible, with no corners. Take your time here, as it's important to get the shape as good as possible—it doesn't have to be 100% accurate, but it will help visually if this *Line* closely follows the same shape. Use the *Left* or *Right Viewport* to make sure that your *Line* is created correctly.

Creating the Chain *Line*

Create the *Line,* which represents the shape of the completed chain. This will be the object that the geometry conforms to exactly, so it's important to get this as accurate as possible. Remember to set the *Initial Type* to *Smooth* and keep the *Drag Type* to *Bezier;* this will allow us to create the *Line* without any corners, creating a smooth flow throughout.

CREATE TAB > SHAPES > LINE

As the *Line* has been created in the center of the chains, we need to move it to one side and position it in the center of the chain geometry that is already there. Once it is in place, duplicate the *Line* and move it to the opposite side—we need to rig both chains on either side, even though they will function exactly the same. Drop those *Lines* under *OBJNAME OBJ_norah1Cogs_LOC* so that they sit in the hierarchy, and rename them as needed (Figure 6.7).

With the *Lines* created, we now need to edit the chain geometry. I'm simply going in there, removing the *Skin Modifier,* dropping it into *sub-object mode,* and deleting everything except one chain link. Now that I have just one chain link, I am going to duplicate this 10 times in *X* so I end up with one long chain. Attach those new chain links to the original chain link, and you should be left with one long chain.

Duplicate this chain again so we have one chain for either side. Finish the editing of the geometry by renaming both chains appropriately. It's time to get that geometry to stick to the *Line* guides that we just created.

Select one of the chains and add a *PathDeform (WSM)* modifier to the geometry. Click the *Pick Path* button to highlight it and then choose either the left or right *Line*—whichever makes most sense from your naming. This will adapt the geometry, but it may not be the desired effect that we want just yet. To fix this up, change the *Path Deform Axis* to another axis until the deformation is correct. From there, hit the *Move to Path* button to jump the geometry over the *Line*.

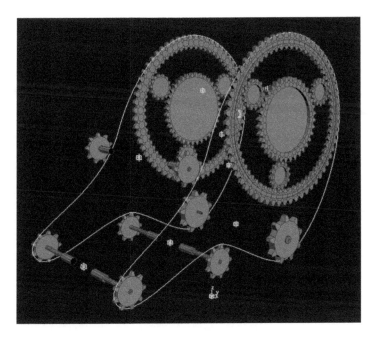

Figure 6.7

Lines act as guides for the chains, which they will end up following exactly.

Repeat this same process for the opposite side, and things should start to look pretty great (Figure 6.8).

If you get close to the geometry, you may notice that there is some squashing and stretching to it, changing its shape as it follows the path that we have assigned to it. This is obviously not realistic, but as I mentioned before, we're going for something that looks great and doesn't need to be 100% accurate. Again, this could be an issue for very realistic product demonstrations that may require 100% accuracy, but for us, this is an acceptable flaw that doesn't really affect the visuals of the train. Oh, and you have some overlapping elements that we really need to fix. To do this, just manipulate the *Stretch* parameter on the *PathDeform (WSM)* modifiers and find the right setting.

Adding a *PathDeform (WSM)* Modifier

Adding a *World-Space Modifier (WSM)* is exactly the same as adding any other kind of modifier. However, these *WSM Modifiers* calculate from the scene-space rather than the object-space.

```
[SELECT OBJECT] > MODIFIERS > WORLD-SPACE MODIFIERS > PATH DEFORM
BINDING (WSM) > [ADJUST PARAMETERS]
```

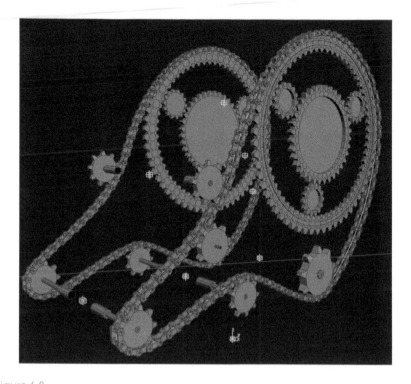

Figure 6.8

The geometry is now deformed correctly and sitting on the *Line,* which has become the *path* for this object.

You may have noticed that some *keyframes* have been added to the geometry, but you can check this by grabbing the geometry and looking at the *TimeSlider—keyframes* will be indicated by colored bars. You can see the effect of these by *scrubbing* the *TimeSlider*. This may look pretty great, but we want to control this movement ourselves; rather, we want our animators to control this movement, so we have to remove these *keyframes* that have been automatically set by Autodesk 3ds Max. So, set your *TimeSlider* to *Frame 0*, select the geometry, highlight those *keyframes,* and hit *delete*. We can now control this ourselves.

To control the movement of the chains, we need to manipulate the *Percent* parameter. If you click and drag the *spinner* from that attribute, you can see that it moves the chain around the path that we have set up. Because this is just an attribute on the *modifier,* we can use *Wire Parameters* to influence it directly. Use a *one-way* connection from *OBJ_norah1Cogs_cog1_LOC.RotateX* to the *Percent on Wire* parameter of the *PathDeform (WSM)* modifier attached to the geometry.

With that connection made, you'll probably notice that although it is not affected by the movement of the cogs, the actual position and movement do not line up correctly. There's no need to fear—all we have to do is add a little bit of math to the *Expression* area in the *Wire Controllers* dialog box and everything will be fixed:

$$-X\_Rotation/4.5$$

Everything is looking great now, but there's one thing that's still broken, although you wouldn't notice it just by looking! Grab the *OBJ_norah1_layout_ CTRL,* and then move and rotate it. You'll see that some crazy deformations are happening to the chains, and they don't look good at all (Figure 6.9).

What we have here is what is known as *double transformation.* A double transformation effect is where an object is subject to transformation data of more than one object (other than its direct parent). This often results in extreme and undesirable shape changes, which is what we're experiencing here. This often happens when we start *skinning,* but it also happens when we introduce *WSMs* to a setup that has multiple parents, just like our *NORAH* rig. Luckily, there's an easy fix for this problem.

Take hold of one of the chains, and in the *Modify Tab,* find the *modifier* named *LinkedXForm.* With this *modifier* added, we need to give it an *XForm* or *Transform* to actually link to. Simply click the *Pick Control Object* button and select the corresponding *Line* object—either *OBJ_norah1Chains_L_LINE* or *OBJ_ norah1Chains_L_LINE.* Now when we move or rotate the train, the chains react

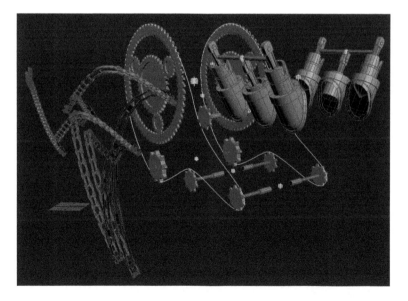

Figure 6.9

Crazy chain deformations need to be fixed before we call this component complete.

as they should. Do the same for the chain on the other side, and we can leave this component alone—it's finished!

6.1.6.3 Pistons

Technically, the pistons form part of the engine (which doesn't really exist), so they should really move before the cogs do. But, this is 3ds Max and not real life, so we can work any way that we want. With that said, it will actually be *OBJ_norah1Cogs_cog1_LOC* driving the pistons, as I've designated that cog as the master and commander of everything automated in this rig (if you haven't noticed already).

We can break a piston into three separate elements, and I'm sure that they have some very specific names, but knowing them really isn't necessary for us, so I'll just use the following:

- Bottom
- Middle
- Top

The bottom section is both where the piston rotates from and the location at which we can move the piston as a full rig—its *ROOT*. The middle one is connected to the bottom and moves along with its rotation, but it keeps its alignment pointed toward the top. This top section keeps its own orientation but moves with the middle section. Please refer to Figure 6.10 for further clarity.

You'll notice that I'm not using the geometry of the *NORAH* model just yet. This allows us to create a piston setup that we can duplicate for each piston that we need to create. It saves us time and makes things much easier to understand…

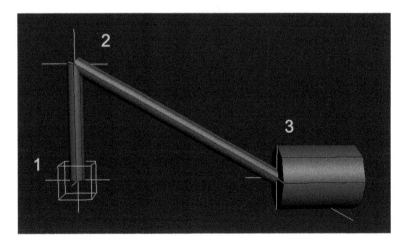

Figure 6.10

A piston is broken into three segments—(1) bottom, (2) middle, and (3) top.

Anyway, as with everything in 3ds Max, there are a number of ways to approach things, and these pistons are no exception. In general, there are two main ways in which to rig a piston—the easy way and the correct way. Let me show you the easy way first because it's very simple and may help you with more basic setups that you may do later.

To start the easy rig, we need to create four *Point Helpers:* the first, positioned where the bottom section is going to rotate from; the second, where the middle needs to be attached (at the end of the bottom section); the third, in the same place as the second; and finally, the fourth at the top.

With the *Point Helpers* set, use the *Select and Link* tool to link the middle *Point Helpers* (2 and 3 in the figure) to the bottom *Point Helper* (1). Quickly switch to the *Hierarchy Tab* and click the *Link Info* button. Make sure that one of the middle *Point Helpers* is selected, and under the *Inherit* rollout, disable *Rotate X, Y,* and *Z*. Now, when you rotate the bottom *Point Helper,* that middle *Point Helper* will move but not rotate. Link the last *Point Helper* (4) to this edited *Point Helper.*

Now add a *LookAt constraint* to the other middle *Point Helper* and aim it at the top *Point Helper* (4). Rotate the bottom *Point Helper* once again, and if you notice the middle *Point Helper* twisting, you will need to adjust its *LookAt Axis.* To do this, access the *Motion Tab,* and on the *LookAt Constraint* rollout, look under *Select LookAt Axis.* Rotating the bottom *Point Helper* now should give the correct and desired results.

Changing Object Inheritance

By changing the transformations that an object inherits, we can drastically change how an object transforms in three-dimensional (3D) space (Figure 6.11).

```
[SELECT OBJECT] > HIERARCHY TAB > LINK INFO > INHERIT > [TOGGLE
OPTIONS]
```

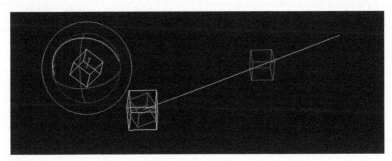

Figure 6.11

This is the easy way to rig pistons. Changing an *Object's Transform Inheritance* can change the way in which an object moves, rotates, or scales dramatically.

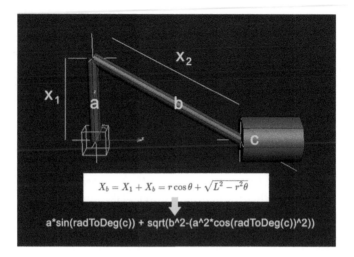

Figure 6.12

Trigonometry is used to make sure that the piston rig behaves correctly, and as we expect it to.

This easy way should be working just great right now, but by using the *Object Inheritance* as a way of limiting object *transformations*, we will run into some problems. One issue in particular is when we try to rotate the rig. That one object piece, which we have limited, will not behave as we would expect an object to if it is in this kind of hierarchical structure. Sadly, there is no real way around this, except to use mathematics to solve the problem (Figure 6.12).

By using some trigonometry, we can evaluate the rotation of the piston and accurately calculate where the end of the piston should be at all times. But, the first thing we need to do is create a basic piston setup, which we can apply the math to. Using Figure 6.13 as reference, we need to use both *Point Helpers* and *Cylinders* to re-create this piston. Here's the hierarchy that I'm using for this part of the rig:

- OBJ_norah1piston_RIG_001 (Point Helper)
  - OBJ_norah1piston_RIG_002 (Point Helper)
    - OBJ_norah1piston_RIG_003 (Cylinder)
- OBJ_norah1piston_RIG_004 (Point Helper)
  - OBJ_norah1piston_RIG_005 (Cylinder)
- OBJ_norah1piston_RIG_006 (Point Helper)
  - OBJ_norah1piston_RIG_007 (Cylinder)

Add a *LookAt Constraint* to *OBJ_norah1piston_RIG_005* so that it is aimed at *OBJ_norah1piston_RIG_006*. With the hierarchy created, we now need to convert the mathematical formula into something that 3ds Max can understand. We'll be using an *Expression Controller* to drive the *X Position* of the *OBJ_norah1piston_RIG_006* element.

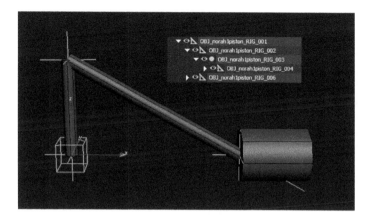

Figure 6.13

The hierarchy of the piston rig.

Adding an *Expression Controller*

Adding an *Expression Controller* to an object allows us to add expressions to the chosen *transform*.

```
[SELECT OBJECT] > MOTION TAB > PARAMETERS > ASSIGN CONTROLLER >
[CHOOSE TRANSFORM] > ASSIGN CONTROLLER > FLOAT EXPRESSION
(Figure 6.14)
```

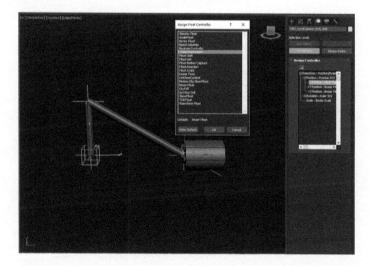

Figure 6.14

Adding an *Expression Controller* to an object is relatively easy.

With the *Expression Controller* dialog box open, we need to add the following expression, which is converted from the mathematical formula discussed earlier:

$$a*sin(radToDeg(c)) + sqrt(b^2-(a^2*cos(radToDeg(c))^2))$$

For this to work correctly, we need to first create three *Scalar variables,* which should be entered as *Controllers* and not *Constants:*

1. a = $OBJ_norah1piston_RIG_003.Height
2. b = $OBJ_norah1piston_RIG_005.Height
3. c = $OBJ_norah1piston_RIG_002.rotation.controller."Y_Rotation"

With those variables entered, and now that we've made sure that we're affecting the correct object and *transform,* we just have to enter the expression here into the *Expression* area of this *Expression Controller* and hit *Evaluate.* Boom! We have a working piston rig that uses mathematics, and no matter how we rotate the full rig, it will always work as expected. Woohoo! (See Figure 6.15.)

We now have to duplicate this rig for each of the pistons on the *NORAH* model and attach things correctly. That's a simple case of setting an initial rotation for each of the piston rigs and changing the *Height* of the *Cylinder* objects and then

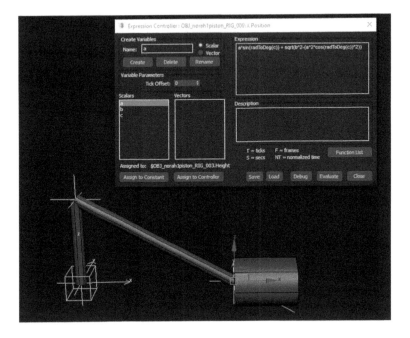

Figure 6.15

The completed piston rig works correctly, no matter which angle it rotates to.

6. Animation and Automation Rig: Part 1

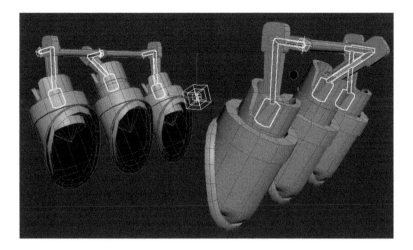

Figure 6.16

The piston rig is correctly positioned and linked to the main geometry.

parenting the *Point Helpers* or using a *Link Constraint* so that the actual pistons follow along correctly with our rig. It's a little time consuming, but it's worth it to have a great-looking piston rig (Figure 6.16).

To get everything turning and working together, use the *Wire Parameters* tool to wire a connection so that the *OBJ_norah1Cogs_cog1_LOC* object drives the rotation of the pistons. You may want to multiply the rotation amounts for the pistons so they will look even better when animated, but I'll leave that choice up to you.

6.1.6.4 Wheels

As with every other automated movement in this rig, the wheels are driven directly from the *OBJ_norah1Cogs_cog1_LOC* (Figure 6.17). I'll go over this pretty quickly,

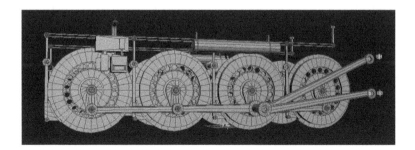

Figure 6.17

The main wheels for this carriage are driven with *Wire Parameters* as usual.

as I'm sure you're already super-skilled with the *Wire Parameters* tools by now! (I think that this takes the award for the smallest subheading in this book…of I stop writing in here of course.)

Yeah, there's nothing else to say about the wheels. Moving on!

6.1.6.5 Beams

The beams attached to the wheels of this carriage don't require anything complicated. Because the geometry is affected by the *Point Helpers* that we already have in place, we just need to add *LookAt Constraints* to allow them not only to turn with the rotation of the wheels, but also to keep their correct alignments.

Add a *LookAt Constraint* to *OBJ_norah1Wheels2_beam_R_LOC* aimed at *OBJ_norah1Wheels3_beam_R_LOC*, and another *LookAt Constraint* between *OBJ_norah1Wheels3_beam_R_LOC* and *OBJ_norah1Wheels4_beam_R_LOC*. That's really all there is to it. Now the beams move along and are aligned as expected when the wheels are turned. All that we need to do for this section is to sort out those side pistons that aren't functioning just yet.

6.1.6.6 Side Pistons

The side pistons work exactly the same way as the main pistons on the upper section of this carriage. However, this time, we're only going to need two piston setups placed in the center of the train, as we will use those two piston setups to drive both sets of side pistons. I know, we're economizing so well right now!

OK, so grab another two piston setups, either by merging in the premade file or by duplicating pistons already in the scene. You could also just re-create another couple of pistons, but wow, that would be the hard way.

With the two pistons ready, we need to make sure that they are positioned and oriented correctly. Then we need to adjust the length of the piston sections so they match up with the lengths of the beams and the distance between where the wheel rotates and the start of the beams. We also need to jump in and adjust the expression that we have, which drives the piston. This is due to both pistons not starting at the same rotation angle. It's no big deal—just a few clicks and a quick calculation, and everything works out fine. Look at Figure 6.18 to see what we end up with.

Fix things up by linking the *Point Helpers* from the actual geometry to our newly created central piston rigs. Then just make sure that those rigs are added into the main hierarchy.

6.1.6.7 Budge Wheels

After all the rigging we've just done, these budge wheels are really easy. We need to connect the rotations of each wheel to (you guessed it) the *OBJ_norah1Cogs_cog1_LOC* so that they turn when everything else moves. Well, you know the drill! Use *Wire Parameters* to wire a *one-way connection* so that the wheels actually turn. You've probably noticed that these wheels are tiny, so add some extra spins by

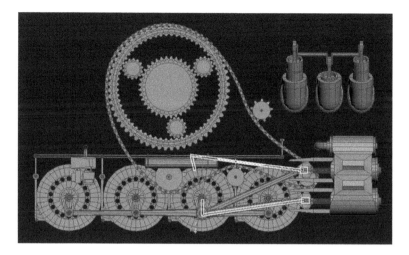

Figure 6.18

Two new piston rigs have been added and adjusted so that they match up correctly with the beams and the distance between the wheel rotation point and the beams themselves. The expressions also have been adjusted slightly to achieve the correct starting angle for the rotations.

multiplying the expression by whatever number looks right. That should give the wheels more movement, as they are going to be spinning quicker than the wheels in the central section. With the wheels ready, give yourself a high-five—you've completed the main components of the first carriage. Congratulations!

6.2 Memory Refresh

See Table 6.1.

Table 6.1 Memory Refresh: Animation and Automation Rig: Part 1

CREATING A LINK CONSTRAINT
```
[SELECT OBJECT] > ANIMATION MENU > CONSTRAINTS > LINK CONSTRAINT
```
CREATING A LINE (FOR THE CHAIN)
```
CREATE TAB > SHAPES > LINE
```
ADDING A PATHDEFORM (WSM) MODIFIER
```
[SELECT OBJECT] > MODIFIERS > WORLD-SPACE MODIFIERS > PATH DEFORM
 BINDING (WSM) > [ADJUST PARAMETERS]
```
CHANGING OBJECT INHERITANCE
```
[SELECT OBJECT] > HIERARCHY TAB > LINK INFO > INHERIT > [TOGGLE OPTIONS]
```
ADDING AN EXPRESSION CONTROLLER
```
[SELECT OBJECT] > MOTION TAB > PARAMETERS > ASSIGN CONTROLLER > [CHOOSE
 TRANSFORM] > ASSIGN CONTROLLER > FLOAT EXPRESSION
```

6.3 Summary

Congratulations! Carriage No. 1 of our complex *NORAH* rig is ready. Even with us preparing things at the *Base Rig* phase, things here were technical, difficult and time consuming—but you did it. I hope that you are proud of yourself because this was a huge accomplishment, and it's behind us now.

Carriages Nos. 2, 3, and 4 are thankfully a lot less taxing, but they still have some intricacies that are going to require attention. Additionally, once we've completed the rigs for each of the separate carriages, we have to get them all working together…but that's in the next chapter. Let's take a break for a moment, and I'll catch up with you in the upcoming pages.

7

Animation and Automation Rig

Part 2

Part 2 of the Animation and Automation rig requires the same level of effort as part 1, but we're working with relatively less complicated elements. In fact, as we work through each of the carriages, from two to three and three to four, things become easier with each step. The *NORAH* model was planned like this, and it works out pretty nicely overall.

As with the previous chapter, we'll be breaking things down by each component of each carriage. Again, this just helps to break down the complexities of the rig itself into more manageable sections. Let's not waste any more time and get straight into the rigging.

7.1 *NORAH*: Carriage No. 2

Our second carriage contains what we can assume is the fuel for the engine on the first carriage (Figure 7.1), delivered by a weird-looking spherical object, hanging from suspension rods and held down by chains. Fuel is fed through the large tubes at the top of the sphere to entrances on the first carriage.

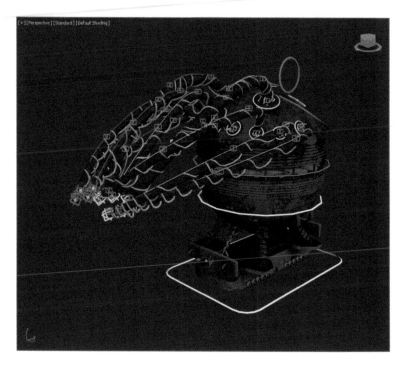

Figure 7.1

NORAH—the Carriage No. 2 element breakdown for rigging.

We start rigging this carriage by using a *Link Constraint* on the *BRANCH* node and layout controller. This fixes up the overall positioning and rotation of the second carriage and sets us up nicely to start breaking down the components.

7.1.1 Tender

The tender, that big sphere holding all the fuel for the steampunk train, is what we'll rig up next. The first thing that we need to do is make sure that the bottom controller has an effect on the geometry. Using the *Link Constraint* as usual, we can link the *Point Helper* that controls the main mass of this object to *OBJ_norah2Tender_LWR_CTRL*. While we're here, we may as well do the same thing to the upper section and *OBJ_norah2Tender_UPR_CTRL*. This allows us to manipulate the main areas and mass of this carriage, and it even gives us the opportunity to break this section apart if we want—good stuff! (See Figure 7.2.)

7.1.1.1 Fans

The three fans featured as part of the tender are driven automatically, just like all of the cogs from the first carriage. Feel free to use any controller or locator you want to give these fans automatic rotation—it really doesn't matter, so long as you wire the parameters correctly. If you would like the fans to spin faster, simply

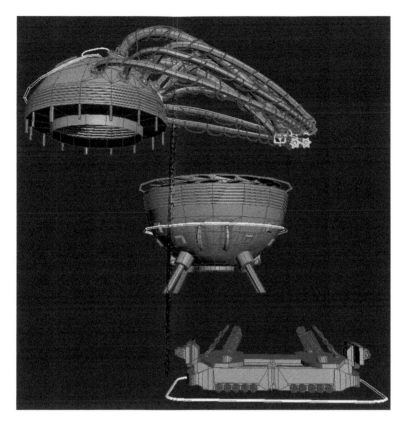

Figure 7.2

The controls here allow us a great amount of flexibility in control and also allow us to move sections apart if we need to.

multiply by a number great than 1 in the *expression* area of the *Wire Parameters* window. I also took the liberty of adding a minus (−) sign to the fan on the right, which allows it to spin in the opposite direction as the one on the left (Figure 7.3).

7.1.1.2 Suspension Rods

The suspension rods could be another one of those areas that we spend a lot of time either making sure that things are working perfectly, or faking things so that they look great, but technically don't really work as they would in the real world. If this was going to be a big focal point of the rig, I'd be tempted to do something more complicated, but since these suspension rods are anchored by chains, they shouldn't move too much—so let's fake it!

We'll use the same technique that we used on the bumper from the first carriage. We'll use some specific *skin weights* to simulate the squash and stretch of the springs. Because these springs are set at an angle, using this method will never

Figure 7.3

It's no big deal to get the fans to rotate automatically—just remember that you can change the speed of the rotations in the *expressions* area of the *Wire Parameters* window.

be perfect, but it should be good enough to create the illusion that this suspension actually works. We'll be blending each of the springs from top to bottom, making sure that there is a clean transition throughout the *skin weights* (Figure 7.4).

7.1.1.3 Chains

The chains help to hold the tender onto the bogie, and they should provide stability to the big sphere that contains whatever futuristic fuel is in there! Just like the suspension rods, there's an easy way or a hard way to rig this—in this case, we'll be taking the easy way, as the hard way is overkill.

Actually, there are a number of ways we could do this, not just two! We could use dynamics—something that would give us very impressive and accurate results. But it is a nightmare to control, and getting it to run in real time, in the viewport, is an overly complex task for what we need. We could go with skinning, exactly as we did with the suspension rods, and while this would work, it would

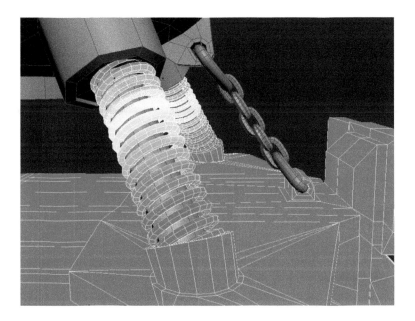

Figure 7.4

Skin Weights are used to simulate the squash and stretch of the springs on these suspension rods.

require us to spend more time *skinning* things, and even then, the geometry may start to tear if we're not perfect with those *skin weights*. We could keep going with the various options we have available, but let's jump into the setup...

Using the locators already in place for the upper and lower sections of the chains, we can use them as guides to run a *Spline* between them. This *Line* object is going to have two *vertices*, one placed at either *Point Helper*. From there, we rename these *Lines* correctly and parent them into the bogie's hierarchy. From there, we can right-click the *Lines* and convert them to an *Editable Spline*. This gives us access to their *sub-object* mode, which is exactly what we need to do.

Converting to *Editable Spline*

Converting any object into an editable version of itself gives us access to many options that are normally locked and hidden from us. Converting to an *Editable Spline* is no different to converting to anything else—simply select the object, right-click it, and convert. Edits to *sub-object* levels are then accessible from the *Modify Tab*.

[SELECT OBJECT] > RIGHT-CLICK > CONVERT TO ... > EDITABLE SPLINE

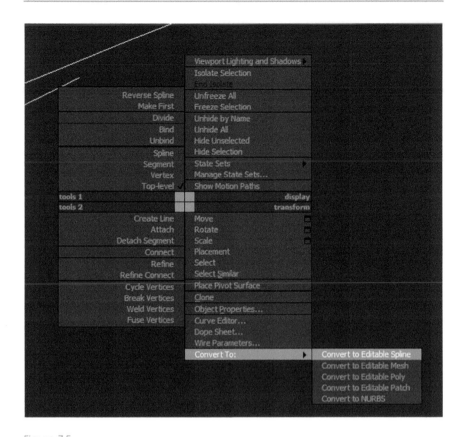

Figure 7.5

Convert the *Lines* into *Editable Splines* and drop into their *sub-object* mode from the *Modify Panel*.

In the object's *Modify Panel*, click on *Vertices* and select just the top *vertex* (Figure 7.5). Use the *Modify Panel's Drop-Down List* and apply the *LinkedXForm* modifier. This will apply the modifier only to our *sub-object* selection, the upper *vertex* that we selected previously. All that we need to do now is press the *Pick Control Object* button and attach it to *OBJ_norah2ChainFront_UPR_LOC* or *OBJ_norah2ChainFront_UPR_LOC*, depending on whether it's the front or back section that you're currently working on.

Change the *skinning* of the chain's geometry to use just the newly created *Lines,* and that should complete the setup. Now when we move the *OBJ_ norah2Tender_LWR_CTRL,* the chain is linked to both the tender and the bogie. Of course, this is not 100% accurate, and you will notice some stretching, but these chains should not be moving enough for an audience to be able to tell that it's not perfect.

Using Linked Transforms on Sub-Objects

Linked XForm modifiers allow us to connect the transforms of one object to another. This can allow one object to affect another, or it can be used to fix double-transformation problems. Additionally, by first dropping into the *sub-object* mode of an element in our scenes, we are able to affect only specific parts of an object, which allows some pretty great options when it comes to using this modifier.

```
[SELECT OBJECT] > [SELECT SUB-OBJECT ELEMENTS] > MODIFY TAB >
LINKED XFORM > PICK CONTROL OBJECT > [SELECT OBJECT AS CONTROL]
```

7.1.1.4 Tubes/Hoses

The tubes/hoses that go from this carriage into the first carriage share a similar kind of setup to the chains that we just rigged. However, they will require a bit more work in getting the *Lines* conforming properly, and we need an additional *modifier* to get things moving as we need them to do.

To conform the *Line* objects correctly, we can use the *Grid and Snapping Setting* to snap to *Vertex* points on the actual geometry. This allows us to run a *Line* from the beginning of the tubes/hoses to the end by snapping the *CVs* of the *Line* at the beginning, middle, and end.

Editing the *Grid* and *Snap* Settings

The Angle Snap Toggle (A) tool can be found on the main interface of Autodesk 3ds Max. Right-clicking this button brings up the *Grid and Snap Settings* window, where we have a number of options that we can change and choose among.

```
RIGHT-CLICK ANGLE SNAP TOGGLE (A) > [EDIT OPTIONS]
```

We need to do this for each of the tubes/hoses in this model. It's important to note that the middle point of the *Line* is going to be put wherever you decide to place that middle *CV*. Its placement should be somewhere that allows the created *Line* to conform to the geometry as closely as possible. In fact, there is nothing wrong with adding as many *CVs* as you want—just remember that the more you add, the more complicated this setup becomes. It also may become too complicated to get great animation results from doing this, so experiment a little and see what feels best. After some trial and error, I decided to use four *CVs* for my setup on this model (Figure 7.6).

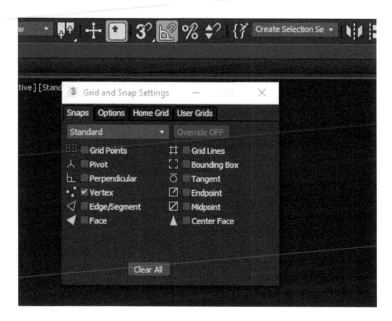

Figure 7.6

By using the *Grid and Snap Settings* to allow us to snap to just the *Vertex* points of the geometry, we can run a *Line* object along the length of the tubes/hoses.

To get these *Lines* to have an effect on the geometry of the tubes/hoses, we just need to add the *Skin* modifier to the geometry and assign a 100% weight value that corresponds with each *Line*. The *Skin* modifier is so versatile that it allows us to use *Lines* or any other kind of object to affect another using the same *skinning* principles that we are accustomed to. I find this extremely helpful, and it works great in this situation.

Now that the geometry is affected by our *Lines,* we need to some kind of control over the *Lines* themselves. To do this, I'm going to be using the *Spline IK Control* modifier. This shouldn't be confused with adding a *Spline IK* system from the *Animation Menu,* as they behave a tiny bit differently. So, take hold of one of the *Lines* and add the *Spline IK Control* modifier to it.

You may notice that nothing much has happened just yet, and that is because we need to tell this modifier what kind of control setup we would actually like. With the *Line* selected, and in the *Modify Tab,* you have control over what the controls are going to look like in the viewport under the *Helper Display* section. I usually leave this as it is, but you do have options if you want to change the visual display of the objects that will be created to control this setup. Above this section is the *Link Types* area. For this setup, I'm choosing *No Linking,* so that each of the *helper objects* that are going to be created behave independently from each other. With this option checked, it's a simple case of hitting that *Create Helpers* button to set up the controls.

Adding a Spline IK Control to Objects

Spline IK systems can be added from the *Animation Menu;* however, we also have the option of creating this kind of control using the *Spline IK Control* modifier. This is sometimes helpful when we want a similar kind of control to a *Spline IK* system but want to be able to access additional options and have more flexibility over this tool.

```
[SELECT OBJECT] > MODIFY TAB > SPLINE IK CONTROL
```

Those controls should now affect the *Line* when they are manipulated. The geometry also should be affected due to the *Skin* modifier we added earlier. To finish this setup, use a *Link Constraint* on those newly created control objects and link them to the actual controllers for the rig. Because I have four controllers for each tube/hose, I'm linking two to the starting controller and two to the end controller, which gives me the kind of control that I want over these tubular hoses! (See Figure 7.7.)

7.1.2 Bogie

As the bogie itself is solid, the only moving parts are the microwheels, which allow it to roll along a track, and the joiners on the front and rear. I'm sure you're already guessing that we need to use *Wire Parameters* once again for the wheels! So automate their rotations by using that *Wire Parameters* tool, and include a multiplication in the *expression* so that they rotate faster than the other wheels in this train's setup, as they are the smallest.

The joiners on this carriage require no special attention. Refer to how we rigged the joiner on the first carriage for information on this. Really, we're not doing anything different here at all.

7.2 *NORAH*: Carriage No. 3

This carriage is explosive…actually, I'd guess that the first three carriages are combustible due to all of that futuristic fuel, but Carriage No. 3 has an actual bomb on board (Figure 7.8). Thinking about things, I'm pretty sure that this is a huge safety risk, as the fourth carriage is meant to contain passengers from the general public…But hey—this is the steampunk future, where nobody cares about that sort of stuff. It just has to look cool!

Okay, stop goofing around. This carriage is pretty straightforward, and as with each carriage, the first thing to do is to use a *Link Constraint* on the *BRANCH* node and the layout controller. Once that is rigged, we can jump into the various components.

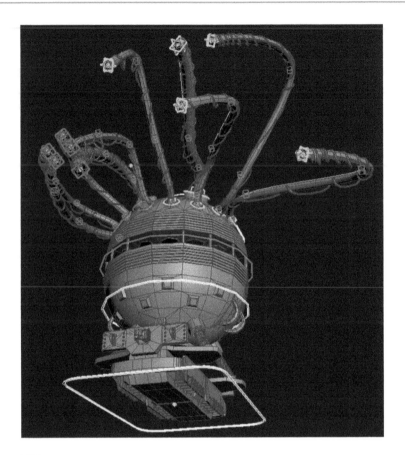

The finished setup for these tubes/hoses shows some great deformations in this section of the rig. Stretching can be seen if inspected closely, but this kind of smooth deformation would be a lot more difficult using another method.

7.2.1 The Frame (Main)

The solid frame on this carriage has its own locator and controller. Although not necessarily needed, it does give us some additional control over the main carriage. As with the *BRANCH* and layout controller, we need to use a *Link Constraint* to make things work. You've probably noticed that this main section also has both a front and rear joiner attached to it, and I don't think I need to reiterate what to do here—so let's get them rigged up.

7.2.1.1 Bomb

Boom!

Sorry, I just had to. There's really no other way to start a "bomb section" without a bang...yeah, there I go again!

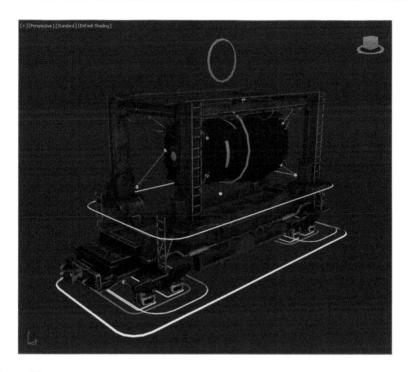

Figure 7.8

NORAH—the Carriage No. 3 element breakdown for rigging.

Uh, OK, so the bomb is a simple case of using a *Link Constraint* on a *Point Helper* and attaching that to the controller kind of setup, just like we're so used to doing now. The only other complexity in this rig are the eight chains that attach the bomb to the frame of the carriage. We already covered rigging chains during the second carriage, and we'll be repeating the exact same steps here. This includes a *Line* created for each of the chains that is parented to the *BRANCH* node and is created from the frame to the bomb. These *Shapes* are named correctly and then converted to an *Editable Spline*. From there, we can drop into *sub-object* mode and select the *vertex* closest to the bomb. With the selection made, we add a *LinkedXForm* modifier to it and attach it as needed (Figure 7.9).

Now, if we move the bomb, each of the chains stretches along with it. Remember that there shouldn't be too much movement in this area, so a small amount of geometry stretching is not going to be something that an audience will notice.

7.2.2 Front and Rear Budges

The front and rear budges have an identical setup of that of the rear budge from the first carriage. Parent the controllers, use *Link Constraints* to get things work, and that's pretty much all there is to it.

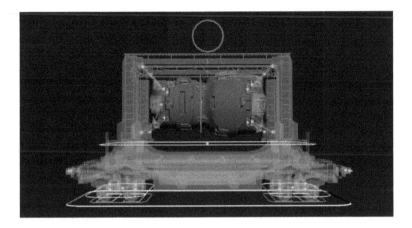

Figure 7.9

That bomb is explosive—I know; I need to stop with the terrible puns that I'm blasting out (groan)!

7.2.2.1 Wheels

As with all the wheel rotations in this rig, things are automated. All that automation stems from the first carriage, so look back over Section 6.1.6.4 in Chapter 6 to set things up correctly. Use *Wire Parameters* to get these wheels moving and add to the *expression* if you think that these wheels need to turn more or less for this setup.

7.3 *NORAH*: Carriage No. 4

Our final carriage is by far the most basic, at least in terms of rigging (Figure 7.10). We have the layout control, the main carriage controller, front and back joiners, front and back budges, and some wheels that need some automation. All the techniques that we need to use have been covered a number of times, and we're actually just duplicating the rigging setups from other carriages. Due to this, I won't go into any details on how to fix up this carriage—I'm more than confident that you know how to rig this.

7.4 Linking Up

Each carriage of our steampunk locomotive now has the necessary rigging elements to allow us to animate the entire train, but we're totally missing out on how all these carriages work together. Oh, and all the carriages are currently sitting on top of one another—that's never going to look great, is it?! (See Figure 7.11.)

Take the layout controllers for the second, third, and fourth carriages and move them backward. Find a logical place for them to be positioned so their

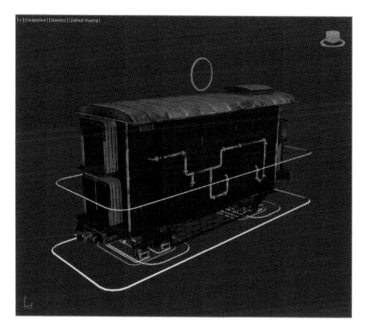

Figure 7.10

NORAH—the Carriage No. 4 element breakdown for rigging.

Figure 7.11

We should probably move these carriages off of each other.

joiners should link together and the tubes/hoses from the second carriage should be close to their insertion points on the first carriage. This should already make things look a whole lot better. The next step is to get these carriages linked.

Create another controller and then duplicate it twice, so that you have three controllers in the scene. These controllers are going to be used for the actual connection between each of the carriages. Position each controller above the rear joiners of the first, second, and third carriages. We now need to edit the *pivot* positions of each of these controllers by lining them up with the joiners. This allows us to pivot from the joiner locations while maintaining the position of our linked controllers (Figure 7.12).

We need to name these newly created controllers correctly, so that they have a place in our rig. Remember that not naming things is really not a good idea! So the names for these controllers are:

- OBJ_norah2_link_CTRL
- OBJ_norah3_link_CTRL
- OBJ_norah4_link_CTRL

I am numbering these from the second carriage, as the first carriage doesn't link to anything because it is the driver for all the other carriages. All right—let's parent things up into the hierarchy. This is going to allow those controllers to have direct control over each of the rigged carriages, kind of grouping this rig together and making it work as one rig rather than four smaller rigs. Use the *Select and Link* tool to link the following controllers:

- OBJ_norah2_link_CTRL to OBJ_norah1_layout_CTRL
- OBJ_norah3_link_CTRL to OBJ_norah2_layout_CTRL
- OBJ_norah4_link_CTRL to OBJ_norah3_layout_CTRL

If we now rotate one of the controllers, things should behave as expected, and moving a carriage's layout controller will have an effect on other carriages.

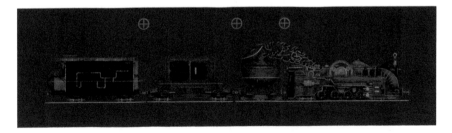

Figure 7.12

Each carriage is now in a logical position, and we have controllers ready to link the carriages together.

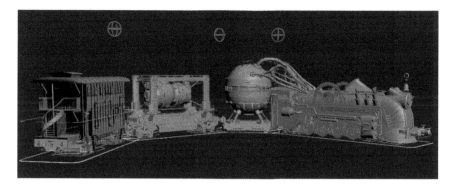

Figure 7.13

Each carriage behaves as we expect, and those tubes/hoses look great while the carriages are manipulated.

Everything works out great, except for those tubes/hoses running from the second carriage to the first. To fix these, all we have to do is use a *Link Constraint* between the controllers on the second carriage and the associated *Point Helper* from the first carriage. We don't want to parent this thing into the hierarchy here, as doing this would move those controls from the second carriage to the first (Figure 7.13).

7.5 The Cleanup Crew

This train rig is a dirty mess at this point, and we need to get a crew in here to clean this thing up! And by "train," I mean the file. And by "crew," I mean us. We've completed the difficult and time-consuming elements of the rigging process required to get our *NORAH* ready for animation. However, there are a few additional tasks that we need to perform to make sure that this rig is cleaned and ready for an actual production.

7.5.1 Hierarchies, Hiding, and Locking

The first thing that needs a cleanup is our rig's hierarchy, and we also need to hide and lock elements that we don't want to be manipulated during animation and production. We should have been keeping the hierarchy of our rig clean as we went through each stage, but sometimes things happen that can make our hierarchies dirty. Be sure to check your hierarchy to make sure that things are in order. You should be able to close up sections of your hierarchy, and everything should appear logically and be parented under one *ROOT* node (Figure 7.14).

With everything sitting in a logical order, we can take sections of our rig easily and hide components that we don't want anyone to edit. What we want to hide are things like locators (*Point Helpers*) and any other rigging-specific nodes, like the *Shapes/Lines* that we created for the chains.

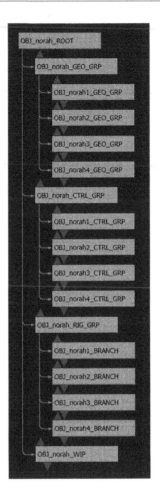

Figure 7.14

A clean and easy-to-navigate hierarchy is an important component of a great rig.

7.5.2 Display Layers

We've neglected the *Display Layers* that we set up a long while ago…OK, well you might not have, but I certainly did. So, now is a good time to go in there and check to make sure that all the objects in the scene are assigned to the correct layers. This shouldn't take too long to get things assigned correctly, and it's a worthwhile task, as after that, we can go in there and adjust the *visibility, rendering,* and *freezing* options for each layer specifically. I know that we've already hidden the objects in the scene, which we don't want to edit or manipulate any further, but this is an additional security measure to hide these things from people, and it takes only a few clicks to fix this up. Remember to just hide everything but the CTRL and GEO layers, then *Freeze* everything but the CTRL layer (Figure 7.15).

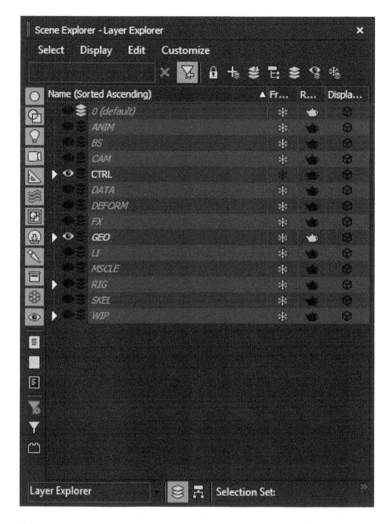

Figure 7.15

Cleaning up those *Display Layers* is quick and easy.

7.5.3 *Display Tab*

While we're on the subject of hiding things from the scene, head on over to the *Display Tab,* and under the *Hide by Category* section, it's advisable to hide everything except the following:

- Geometry
- Shapes
- Helpers

Although we've already hidden everything using the *Display Layers,* this just adds another level of protection from things being seen that we don't want exposed. It's another quick and easy method, but combining both techniques means that our scene is as failure-free as possible (Figure 7.16).

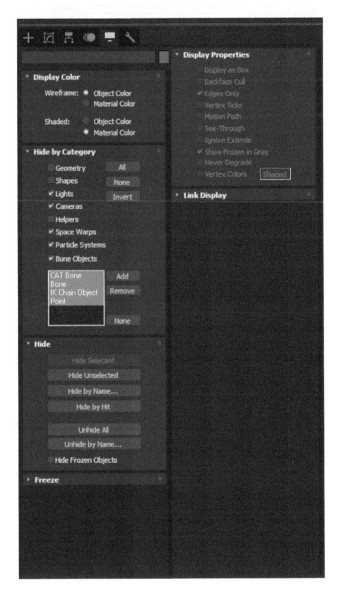

Figure 7.16

The *Display Tab* is another area where we can directly control what is visible in the viewports of our scenes.

7.5.4 Controller Cleaning

Our controllers are in place, and we just need to add the finishing touches so that they are ready for animation. *Freeze Transformations* is the first thing on my list for us to do. This will give us a "zero position, rotation, and scale" value, which is at the default position for the controller. Why is this awesome? Well, if you manipulate the controllers right now, it could be nearly impossible to find that exact default position that the controller starts with. So, grab all the controllers—that's all those *Shapes* that we want the animator to control. With them selected, hold down the *Alt* key and *right-click*. That will bring up a *quad-menu,* and we're going to select the *Freeze Transform* option (Figure 7.17).

This will bring up a new window, which is asking us if we really want to *Freeze Transforms* on the objects that we currently have selected. We do, of course, so hit the *Yes* button! Now we can manipulate our controllers, and instead of having to hit the *Undo* option, we can simply have our controller selected, hit the *Alt* key, and *right-click*. From that *Quad Menu,* we can then just use the *Transform to Zero* option. It's worth noting that this technique simply adds a *Zero Transform* controller to the object that we assign it to. So we could technically add this just like any other *transform controller,* but using the *Quad Menu* is a much easier way of doing things.

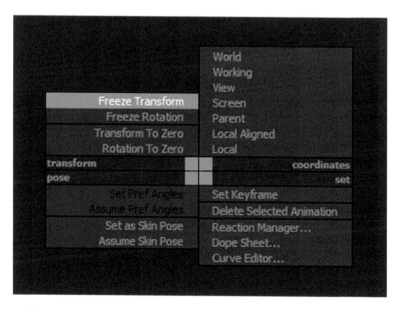

Figure 7.17

Freeze Transforms is a simple process that can really make our controllers a lot easier to work with during animation or other stages during the production.

Freeze Transformations

Freezing Transformations allows us to set zero values for our controllers or other objects in the scene. By doing so, we will have a reference point for the controller, which means that when we set transformation values to zero, the object will jump back to that exact reference position.

```
[SELECT OBJECT] > ALT + RIGHT-CLICK > FREEZE TRANSFORM
```

Transforms are now set to *Zero*, so it's about time that we locked out some of the control options, as we don't want to do just anything and everything with these controllers. What we want to do is to have control over the rig, but not to the point that the rig breaks.

As a general note, the *NORAH* rig is *not* scalable. So at a minimum, we need to lock that scale control away from our controllers. Some controllers just need just movement in one direction, or just the rotate controls on one axis. I'm going to leave the locking and unlocking of control up to your personal preference, as I'm sure you already know what kind of control should be available for each controller that you've created.

To lock out specific transforms, be sure to take hold of the controller first, then head over to the *Hierarchy Tab* and click the *Link Info* button. We've been here before, when we created the piston rig and decided whether objects inherited the movement of others. However, this time, we're interested in the *Locks* area. By turning on the checkboxes for these options, we can effectively lock out that control option for the selected object…and that's really all there is to it!

Locking Object Control

Locking out certain transforms for objects in our scenes can help clarify exactly how an object (or controller) is meant to function. It also allows us to lock out controls for anything that would yield unsatisfactory results in our rigs.

```
[SELECT OBJECT] > HIERARCHY TAB > LOCKS > [EDIT OPTIONS]
```

As a final step, we need to add *Attribute Holders* to our controllers. This is going to hide any of the editable *parameters* that appear in the *Modify Tab* when we select objects (in this case, the controllers) in our scene. It is actually possible for our controllers to share the same *Attribute Holders* by simply selecting multiple *NORAH* rig controllers (if not all of them) and then adding an *Attribute Holder* to them, all at the same time.

It's important to note that objects with a shared *Attribute Holder* also share any *attributes and parameters* that we add to it. In other words, add a *parameter* to an object with a shared *Attribute Holder,* and that *attribute* is going to appear on all

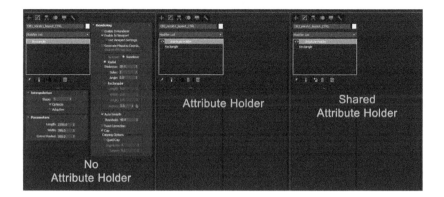

Figure 7.18

The *Modify Tab* for the same controller appears differently if an *Attribute Holder* is assigned to it or not. If the *Attribute Holder* is shared between two objects, its name appears in roman; if it is shared among multiple objects, the name appears in *italics*.

the other objects. This can be a blessing and a curse, but if we wanted *attributes* to appear just on one object, we can simply select just that one object and give it its own *Attribute Holder*. Checking to see if an *Attribute Holder* is shared or not is really simple. Just select the object with the *Attribute Holder* that you want to check, and in the *Modify Tab*, the name *Attribute Holder* will be displayed in *italics* if it is shared (Figure 7.18).

7.6 Memory Refresh

See Table 7.1.

Table 7.1 Memory Refresh: Animation and Automation Rig: Part 2

CONVERTING TO EDITABLE SPLINE

[SELECT OBJECT] > RIGHT-CLICK > CONVERT TO ... > EDITABLE SPLINE

USING LINKED XFORMS ON SUB-OBJECTS

[SELECT OBJECT] > [SELECT SUB-OBJECT ELEMENTS] > MODIFY TAB > LINKED
XFORM > PICK CONTROL OBJECT > [SELECT OBJECT AS CONTROL]

EDITING THE GRID AND SNAP SETTINGS

RIGHT-CLICK ANGLE SNAP TOGGLE (A) > [EDIT OPTIONS]

ADDING A SPLINE IK CONTROL TO OBJECTS

[SELECT OBJECT] > MODIFY TAB > SPLINE IK CONTROL

FREEZE TRANSFORMATIONS

[SELECT OBJECT] > ALT + RIGHT-CLICK > FREEZE TRANSFORM

LOCKING OBJECT CONTROL

[SELECT OBJECT] > HIERARCHY TAB > LOCKS > [EDIT OPTIONS]

7.7 Summary

The Animation and Automation Rig for the *NORAH* asset is now 100% complete—both parts. Congratulations.

By successfully completing this chapter and the previous one, you have created a complex and technical rig that allows both animator and automatic control over various intricate elements. The tips, tricks, and techniques that we've used during these chapters have laid the foundations of knowledge so that you can take this information and apply the methods to your own complicated rigging setups.

What's great about having completed this phase is that we technically don't need to do anything else. That's right! Unlike an organic rig, where we would have to start thinking about *skinning* and *deformers* so that a soft-body setup actually deforms and moves correctly with our rig, we have already taken care of things during these two chapters. As most of our model contains hard-surface geometry, our rig has had to make sure that these elements behave as expected and already are attached correctly to the underlying rigging systems. The small areas that need some kind of deformation have already been taken care of using *skinning* techniques and other methods to get them to deform as we need them to.

This obviously puts into question what the next chapter, about the *Deformation Rig*, is going to cover, but we will get to that in good time. For now, take some time out. Get away from the computer and leave 3ds Max to chill out for a while. Soak in your success for having completed this huge obstacle—you've done something fantastic here.

8

Deformation Rig

As we discussed in the previous chapter, the rig for our *NORAH* asset is technically complete. We can take that finished rig and start using it in production, ending up with a great-looking steampunk locomotive animation. But, in keeping with the 3-Stage-Asset-Build (3SAB) that I stick to, no matter what, we're going to create the final stage—the *Deformation Rig*. Again, this is not technically needed for our mechanical creations, but that doesn't mean we should just give it up and get lazy.

This chapter is going to give us the opportunity to enhance the rig and specific elements and setups that we've already created. Throughout this phase, we have the chance to edit and change parts of the rig where we would like a different kind of setup, output, or both. We're going to spend some time discussing things that we can add to our already-completed rig and challenge specific areas of the existing setup where other techniques might be needed for certain situations. For instance, the term "shot-specific rigs" refers to rigs that are created for use in just one shot or a few shots. These kinds of rigs are not suitable for general production use, but they do allow specific, specialist controls to do one or more things. Currently, our *NORAH* is a more generic rig. It should be good for pretty much all situations, but there may be times when creating setups for specific shots or situations may be needed.

Let's jump in and think about creating some shot-specific rigs for *NORAH*…

8.1 Automated Wheel Rotation

The current setup for our *NORAH* rig requires us to rotate the *OBJ_norah1_drive_ CTRL* controller manually to get the wheels of the train to turn. However, it may be beneficial for us to create a setup whereby the forward translation of the train automates the rotation of the wheels correctly.

To do something like this, trigonometry can be used to calculate the rotation of a wheel (or any kind of circular object) by an amount that corresponds directly to the distance traveled, moved, or translated by another object. In fact, the logic and the math behind this are relatively simple, and all we really need to know is the distance traveled, divided by the radius of the wheel or other circular object that we want to rotate.

Applying this to our rig is also simple, but just so we are completely sure of how it works, let's create an auto-wheel rotation setup on some primitive objects. To start off, create a *Box* and a *Cylinder* from the *Create Tab*. Use the *Select and Link* tool to parent the *Cylinder* to the *Box*. If you haven't already guessed, we're going to be using the position of the *Box* to rotate the *Cylinder*.

We're going to use our friend *Wire Parameters,* so go ahead and *wire* the rotation of the *Cylinder* to the position of the *Box* using a *one-way* connection. Oh, and I know that I'm not telling you which attributes to wire up specifically here—I'm guessing that you can figure out which axis you need for both attributes.

Now that the connection is made, when we move the *Box,* that *Cylinder* is spinning out of control. Remember that bit about using math, and trigonometry specifically? Well, this is where it comes in. We need to add the following equation to the expression in our *Wire Parameters* window:

```
$Box.[X,Y,Z]_Position/$Cylinder.Radius
```

8.1.1 Distance/Radius

In this case, the *Distance* will be the position of our *Box* and the *Radius* will be the actual radius of the *Cylinder*. Once that expression is updated, try moving the *Box* again. You should now have a more accurate rotation of the *Cylinder*. All we need to do now is add this setup to our *NORAH* rig.

Automated Wheel Rotation Using *Distance* and *Radius*

This is a very simple set that uses *Wire Parameters* from a driving object into the object that needs to rotate. Link the rotating object to the driving object, and then create a one-way connection that calculates the *Distance* of the driving object divided by the *Radius* of the rotating object.

```
[RIGHT-CLICK WHEEL] > WIRE PARAMETERS ... > POSITION >
ROTATION > [DISTANCE/RADIUS]
```

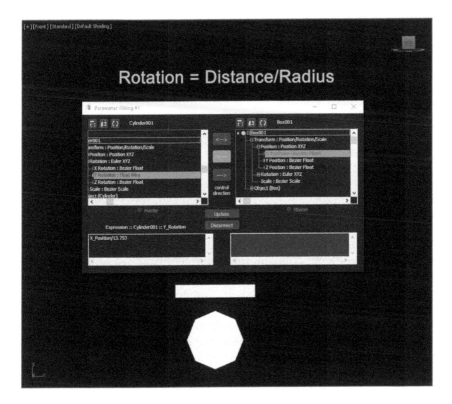

Figure 8.1

By using the equation Distance/Radius when using the *Wire Parameters* tool, we can accurately and automatically drive the wheels of a model based on the distance traveled.

To add this to the *NORAH* rig, the first thing we need to do is find the radius of the wheel that we want to rotate. Remember that *NORAH* has a variety of wheel sizes, so finding the radius for each of these sizes is necessary. An easy way to do this is to create a *Cylinder,* line it up with the wheel that you need to find the measurements for, and then adjust the *Radius* attribute of the *Cylinder.* Once that's done, record the *radius* in your notes and move to the next wheel size (Figure 8.1).

With the measurements in our notes, we can adjust the *Wire Parameters* for each *Point Helper* (locator) that controls the rotation of the wheels. Instead of using the *OBJ_norah1_driver_CTRL,* we're going to use the *OBJ_norah1_layout_ CTRL,* as this is what we will use for the *distance* part of our expression. Okay, so link it up, connect or update it, and there you go. Automated wheel rotation has been granted to our steampunk locomotive. Add this to the train-track rigging that we just did, and we have another shot-specific rig. Woohoo!

8.2 Technically Accurate Chain Rigging

The chain that we rigged during the Animation and Automation phase works great for our *NORAH* rig, but it does have some limitations that could be a deal-breaker in some situations. While the current rig is suitable for most of the results that we need, it also has some undesirable effects, including geometry stretching and making it very difficult to make sure that all the teeth from the cogs fit into the chain perfectly. For the needs of this book, these issues are not really problems, but I realize that you may need something that is more accurate if you are rigging product demonstrations or even technical client videos—I know that they can be extremely demanding. Also, I mentioned during Chapter 6 that I'd share a more accurate way of doing things, so here it is!

We need just one section of the chain link for this setup, and we need to use the same *Line* that we used to trace around the cogs in part 1 of the Animation and Automation rig (described in Chapter 6). Focusing just on the chain link right now, we need to make sure that the pivot of the outer link is in the middle of the object, but the inner link needs its pivot positioned such that the link will pivot from at the start of its geometry. We then need a *Point Helper* that will sit at the start of the outer-link geometry, where the links will pivot from. Once this mini-setup has been completed, we need to make sure that everything is in one hierarchy by using the *Select and Link* tool to link the inner link and the *Point Helper* to the outer link (Figure 8.2).

With that done, implement *Freeze Transforms* on all those objects to make sure that things are as clean as possible. We now need to add a *Path Constraint* to the outer chain link and get it to follow the path that we already created. Turn on

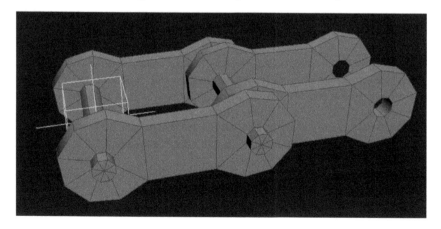

Figure 8.2

We need to spend some time setting up a chain-link section by changing pivot points, adding a *Point Helper,* linking everything together, and *freezing transformations* on all those objects.

the *Follow* option, and remember to delete the *keys* that this *constraint* creates. Use the tools that it provides to flip the geometry as needed for it to sit correctly on the path.

Now we can switch the *percent* controller from a *Linear Float* to a *Float List*, which will allow us to have two *Bezier Float* controllers, with the second one on the list being *Active*, which should be assigned straight away. From there, grab the full chain-link setup and *duplicate* it as an *instance*. Line things up as well as possible, and then *copy* the second *Bezier Float* controller from the first chain link into the first *Bezier Float* of the second chain link. Make sure that this is also an *instance,* and now, as we control the first chain link, the second moves along automatically and as expected.

To make sure that the chain feels linked together, we need to add a *LookAt Constraint* to the inner chain link and get it to aim at the second chain link's *Point Helper*. Repeat this process, and you'll have an accurately rigged chain that doesn't bend or deform incorrectly (Figure 8.3).

Accurate Chain Rigging

Creating an accurate chain rig with a robust setup requires a number of complicated steps. Due to this, it's a little difficult to write a step-by-step process for this box, but I'll try my best:

```
CREATE CHAIN LINK
FREEZE TRANSFORMS
PATH CONSTRAIN (WITH FOLLOW)
PATH.PERCENT = FLOAT LIST
FLOAT LIST = (1) BEZIER FLOAT, (2) BEZIER FLOAT (ACTIVE)
DUPLICATE AND POSITION
INSTANCE (2) BEZIER FLOAT FROM FIRST LINK TO (1) BEZIER FLOAT
  OF SECOND
LOOKAT CONSTRAINT FROM FIRST INNER LINK TO SECOND POINT HELPER
REPEAT TO COMPLETE CHAIN
```

Oh, just one final note on this setup: If you find that the last link doesn't match up and complete the chain correctly, you need to find the length of the *Line* to which the chain is *Path Constrained,* and change that appropriately. It's not a big deal, but I just thought I'd mention it!

8.3 Dynamic Rope and Wires

As we were rigging *NORAH,* you may have noticed that there were a lot of wires coiled around some of the structures, but we never really mentioned them and opted not to rig them, as that would be overkill. However, the rigging of ropes

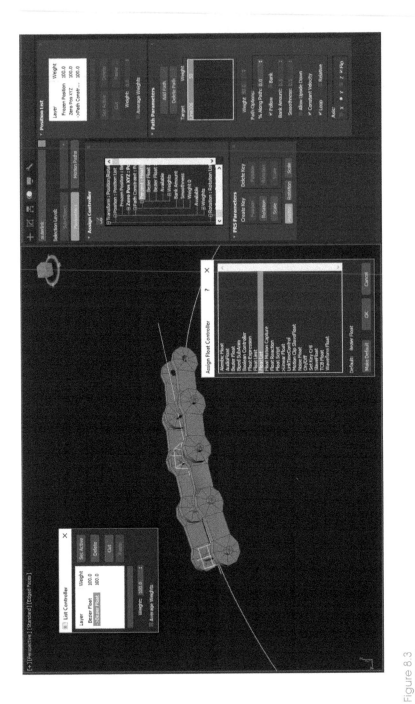

Figure 8.3

Once we have two of the chain links completed, we can duplicate the second chain link to create the rest of the links and complete the chain. Remember to use instances as things are duplicated in order to retain the setup and copied controllers.

and wires is something that often is required when we rig mechanical structures and machinery.

One option for doing this is to use a *Spline* object, just as we did with the tubes/hoses from the second carriage to the first. This is a viable option for many setups, and it allows us to give animators full control over the movements and deformations of ropes and wires on our rigs. Of course, there are times when animating these kinds of objects would be cumbersome or just flat-out frustrating—especially if these objects are just reacting to movements and forces around them. Luckily, we have the option to use dynamics to simulate the secondary motions accurately.

Plug-ins are a great option, and they provide powerful tools for dynamic-based animation. Inside real-time engines, these kinds of systems are often built in. Otherwise, middleware options can be added to the real-time engines. This is all great, but if we want to simulate dynamics in Autodesk 3ds Max, we don't need to worry about any of that—we can just use the built-in dynamics system that we already have access to.

This system is called *MassFX,* and it is a robust dynamics system that can help us when we want to add dynamically driven content to our rigs. It's important to note that the biggest drawback with using this system is that it doesn't run in real time. What I mean by this is that for us to see the dynamics in action, we have to run the dynamic simulation manually. This kind of limitation is often standard with dynamics systems, so I suggest that you keep any dynamics until the end of your rigging setups (like now) and keeping these setups hidden from the animation crew that you may be working with is highly advisable.

Let's add a quick *MassFX* setup to a *Cylinder* that is *skinned* to some *Bones.* I'll let you quickly set that up yourself—just make sure that the *Cylinder* has enough loops in order for it to deform nicely. Once these objects are ready, grab hold of all the *Bones* and head up to the *Animation Menu,* where you should be able to find the *MassFX* area. Look through the options for the *Create Dynamic Ragdoll* option and apply that to the selected *Bones.*

We've now set up a *MassFX ragdoll* system where we can see how our objects have been affected by clicking the *Run Simulation* button on the *MassFX* floating toolbar. You'll notice that the objects are now dynamic and drop straight down to the floor. What we really need for this is some way to anchor at least one section of the *Cylinder* to give the impression that it would be pinned to something.

To pin one of the *Bones* in place, we can use the *Create Universal Constraint* option on the *MassFX* floating toolbar. An area-of-influence marker is now created, and that can be edited as needed. Just select the *Bone* that you would like to pin, hit the *Universal Constraint* option and the *Run Simulation* again. Now you should have a dynamic rope that is pinned from the *Bone* that you selected.

Rigging Rope and Wires Dynamically

MassFX is the built-in dynamics system in 3ds Max, and we can use that to leverage dynamics within the program itself, without having to rely on other applications or plug-ins. It's important to note that, like many dynamics systems, *MassFX* cannot run in real time in our viewports, so once we set up the dynamics, we have to run the simulations manually to see if they work correctly.

```
[CREATE BONES] > [SELECT BONES]
ANIMATION MENU > MASSFX > RIGID BODIES > CREATE DYNAMIC RAGDOLL
CUSTOMIZE > SHOW UI > SHOW FLOATING TOOLBARS
MASSFX TOOLBAR > RUN SIMULATION
[SELECT BONE TO CONSTRAIN/PIN] > MASSFX TOOLBAR > CREATE
 UIVERSAL CONSTRAINT
```

8.4 Rumble and Vibration Controls

Both the second and third carriages of the *NORAH* rig have objects that are suspended by either chains or an actual suspension system (Figure 8.4). These items are the tender, from the second carriage, and the bomb, from the third carriage. At this point, these objects are fully in the animator's realm of control, but wouldn't it be great if these two objects rumbled and vibrated as the train moved automatically? I think it would. Now, don't get me wrong—this is not going to be a big movement by any means, but a subtle jiggle would give these elements a lot of life. I also would like animators to have control over this rumble movement, so they can dial it in as much or as little as they desire. I'd even like for them to be able to animate over the top of this rumbling so that they have full control over the position, rotation, and rumbling for these elements.

We'll start this setup by creating a controller that will control the rumble and vibration for both of the objects that we want to affect. I'm going to be using a *Slider* that will sit on the top of the view at all times. I'm using this because the rumble is very much a secondary control, and we haven't used one in this rig just yet, so why not?! (See Figure 8.5.)

As you can see, I've positioned this controller in the lower-right corner of the screen to make this as unobtrusive as possible in the view of the scene itself. I've also added the *Label Rumble* so that it is obvious what this controller will actually do. Everything else has been left at its default values.

The next step is to add a *Noise Controller* to both the *OBJ_norah2Tender_LWR_CTRL* and the *OBJ_norah3Bomb_CTRL*. However, we need to do this in a specific way so that we are able to retain the ability to move and rotate the controller while it rumbles, shakes, and vibrates. To do this, we need to *Alt + Right-Click Freeze Transforms* so that a *Position List* controller is automatically created, with a *Zero Pos XYZ* added to the active second channel. We then need to go to the *Motion*

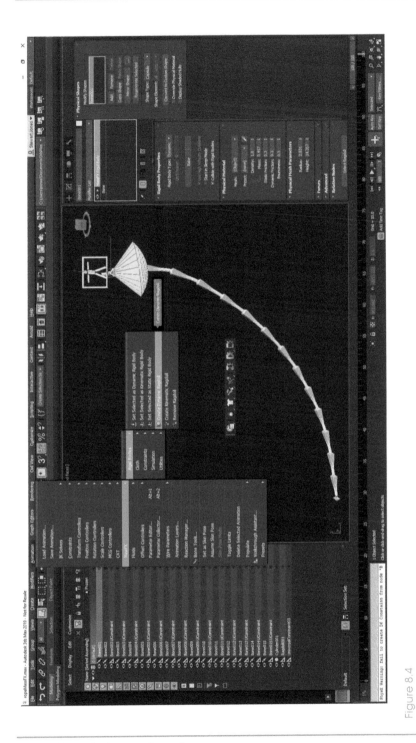

Figure 8.4

Using the built-in dynamics system called *MassFX*, we can create dynamic ropes, among many other dynamic objects.

We'll use a *Slider* manipulator control for the rumble on the two suspended objects.

Tab and find the first channel, which is a *Frozen Position* controller, and change that to the default *Position XYZ* controller (Figure 8.6).

Next, we can expand each of the position controllers and assign a *Noise Float* to each of them, leaving the settings at their defaults. We then go back to our friend, the trusty *Wire Parameters,* to create a one-way connection between the *OBJ_norah_rumble_CTRL.value* to *OBJ_norah2Tender_LWR_CTRL.X Position. Noise Strength.* We also need to do the same for the *Y* and *Z Positions,* as well as the same setup for the *OBJ_norah3Bomb_CTRL* object. Now, when we adjust the *Slider* value, the affected controllers will vibrate and rumble when we hit the *Play* button!

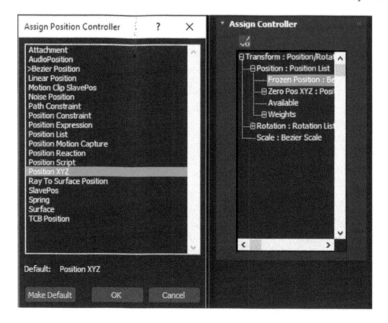

Figure 8.6

Add a *Position XYZ* controller to the first channel on the *Position List* controller.

Adding Noise to Simulate Rumbles and Vibrations

Adding a *Noise Float* to the controller of an object can help us to simulate randomized motion for our objects. If we would like additional control over the movement of the *Noise*, we need to make sure that we are using a *Float List* controller on the object so that we can assign multiple channels. Then one of those channels can be assigned a controller that gives us the option to position the object manually.

```
CREATE TAB > HELPERS > MANIPULATIRS > SLIDER
[SELECT OBJECT] > NOISE FLOAT CONTROLLER
[WIRE PARAMETERS] SLIDER VALUE > NOISE STRENGTH
```

If the output of the *Noise* is not suitable, or if you just want to change the look/animation of the *Noise*, you can go back into the controller settings and adjust some of the values (Figure 8.7). Feel free to consult the 3ds Max help files for more

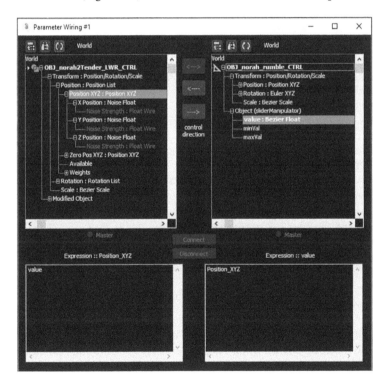

Figure 8.7

We use *Wired Parameters* to drive a *one-way connection* from the *Slider* controller's value into each of the *Noise Controllers* that we have added to *Position X, Y,* and *Z* of the object.

information on the *Noise Controller*, but it's pretty straightforward to understand. In fact, it's more fun just to try the settings that are available and check out what kind of results you can get randomly.

8.5 Memory Refresh

See Table 8.1.

Table 8.1 **Memory Refresh: Deformation Rig**

AUTOMATED WHEEL ROTATION USING DISTANCE AND RADIUS

```
[RIGHT-CLICK WHEEL] > WIRE PARAMETERS ... > POSITION > ROTATION >
 [DISTANCE/RADIUS]
```

ACCURATE CHAIN RIGGING

```
CREATE CHAIN LINK
FREEZE TRANSFORMS
PATH CONSTRAIN (WITH FOLLOW)
PATH.PERCENT = FLOAT LIST
FLOAT LIST = (1) BEZIER FLOAT, (2) BEZIER FLOAT (ACTIVE)
DUPLICATE AND POSITION
INSTANCE (2) BEZIER FLOAT FROM FIRST LINK TO (1) BEZIER FLOAT OF
 SECOND
LOOKAT CONSTRAINT FROM FIRST INNER LINK TO SECOND POINT HELPER
REPEAT TO COMPLETE CHAIN
```

RIGGING ROPE AND WIRES DYNAMICALLY

```
[CREATE BONES] > [SELECT BONES]
ANIMATION MENU > MASSFX > RIGID BODIES > CREATE DYNAMIC RAGDOLL
CUSTOMIZE > SHOW UI > SHOW FLOATING TOOLBARS
MASSFX TOOLBAR > RUN SIMULATION
[SELECT BONE TO CONSTRAIN/PIN] > MASSFX TOOLBAR > CREATE UIVERSAL
 CONSTRAINT
```

ADDING NOISE TO SIMULATE RUMBLES AND VIBRATIONS

```
CREATE TAB > HELPERS > MANIPULATIRS > SLIDER
[SELECT OBJECT] > NOISE FLOAT CONTROLLER
[WIRE PARAMETERS] SLIDER VALUE > NOISE STRENGTH
```

8.6 Summary

The rigging techniques that we've discussed in this chapter can add to and enhance our *NORAH* rig in various ways. They are entirely optional and may be required only for shot-specific needs, but they can be extremely helpful to know about if situations arise where these methods are needed.

The automated wheel rotations using distance and radius calculations can be helpful for many vehicle rigs, and accurate chain rigging can come in handy for any kind of product demonstrations where the chain is the central focus. I still feel that this is an overly complex procedure to do for most situations, but now you can make up your own mind about which techniques will suit your rigs better.

We also covered *MassFX* in this chapter, which is the built-in dynamics system that comes with newer versions of 3ds Max. We have only barely touched the surface of using these tools; whole books could be written on just this topic—and they have! But I hope that this brief introduction to the system will give you an understanding of what is possible, and it may even spark your interest in learning more about that tool, or at least opening up options to you when rigging other assets.

Finally, we added rumble and vibrations to the supported elements in the *NORAH* asset. Once again, this is a completely optional setup, but it is an easy way to add an automated element to the rig that will keep animators from focusing on these sections too much.

There's still so many things we could add to this setup, and even more mechanical rigs that have not been applicable to the *NORAH* asset. Maybe we should take a look at one or two other mechanical setups that could be helpful to us? Yeah, let's do that in the next chapter!

9
More Mechanical Rigging

The *NORAH* asset gave us the opportunity to create a number of technical and complex mechanical setups in order to complete the rig. We then looked at additional rigging techniques that we could use either to completely change the setups that we had already created or to enhance what was already there. Of course, even with all the methods that we covered, there are still many other kinds of mechanical rigs that we haven't had the chance to discuss.

Throughout this chapter, we are going to take some time to explore some rigging methods that could be beneficial in other kinds of situations where mechanical rigs will be needed. We'll take a quick look at various tips, tricks, and techniques that weren't covered during the creation of the *NORAH* rig, but hopefully will come in handy as a helpful reference for other journeys that we may take when rigging in three dimensions (3D)! Because our rigging for the *NORAH* object is now complete, we won't be using that asset for this chapter. Instead, we will be creating some basic geometry to help illustrate the rigging techniques that we are using. From there, these methods can be applied directly to your own mechanical creations.

9.1 Train Tracks

Throughout the rigging of the *NORAH* asset, we didn't discuss the train tracks at all. This was deliberate because we were focusing purely on the setup for the main focus point—the steampunk locomotive itself. It may seem like a big deal to make our train follow along some train tracks, but it is in fact relatively simple. What's great about this setup is that we will use tools and techniques that we've already used and gotten accustomed with, so we should have a good idea of what happening with the track rigging.

The first thing we need is the geometry of the train tracks. I've included a section of train track in the completed *NORAH* asset if you would like to work with something more detailed, but for this example, I'm just going to forget about the geometry for the tracks, as it is a very easy setup that we've created a few times now.

To start off with the train-track rigging, we need a *path* for the train and the track to follow. This is nothing more than a *Line* created from the *Shapes* options. This can be whatever shape you want, but keep in mind that it shouldn't curve too much, as the train won't be able to maneuver on extreme curves if it has only four points on which it can pivot. It's probably worth not including any hills or sloping shapes for this either, just while we are setting up our rig at the beginning. Afterward, we can experiment more.

If you're using geometry for the train tracks, duplicate the track geometry as many times as you need to cover the length of the *path*. *Attach* all that geometry together and use a *PathDeform (WSM)* modifier, just as we did for the chain setup, so that the geometry conforms to the *path* as we expect it to. Remember to delete the *keyframes* that this *modifier* automatically adds to the geometry, as we don't need any movement on our train tracks.

Now, let's get that train onto this track! First, create a *Box* with the *Length, Width, and Height Segs* set to *1* and the actual *length, width,* and *height* set to the length and width of the train that you're putting onto the track, but keep the height small so that it doesn't cover the train geometry. Convert this to an *Editable Poly* and connect the *edges* down the *length* of the *Box* four times. Line up these newly created *Edges* with the joiners of each carriage so that they match the pivot locations of each section of the model (Figure 9.1).

Now create *Point Helpers* and use an *Attachment Constraint* to stick them to the *Box*. We need to position these *Point Helpers* at each *edge* along the *length* of the *Box*—one at the start and end of the *Box* geometry, and the others where the pivots of the separate carriages are. This isn't particularly difficult, but it feels a little clumsy because we have to use the *Set Position* option on the *Attachment Constraint*.

Now we can use a *Position Constraint* on each of the Boxes, or on the controllers of the *NORAH* rig if you're using that, on the first carriage's layout control and the Link controllers of the other carriages. They will need to be constrained to the *Point Helpers* that we just created with the *Keep Initial Offset* checkbox enabled so

Figure 9.1

We should have a *Box* that is the same length and width as the train that we are rigging, but the height should be less so we can still see the geometry of the asset. I'm just using *Boxes* for this example, but I'm keeping the same kind of setup.

that they maintain their original position in the scene. Next, we just need to add a *Lookat Constraint* so that they look at the *Point Helper* behind them. Again, check that the *Keep Initial Offset* checkbox is enabled so that the carriages don't twist and rotate out of place (Figure 9.2).

Finally, we need to add a *PathDeform (WSM)* modifier to the *Box* that spans the length of the train. Select the *path* that we already created when setting the *Pick Path* button, then hit the *Move to Path* button to jump the setup onto the path itself. You may have to spend some time adjusting the *Rotation* and other parameters here, but this shouldn't be too much trouble.

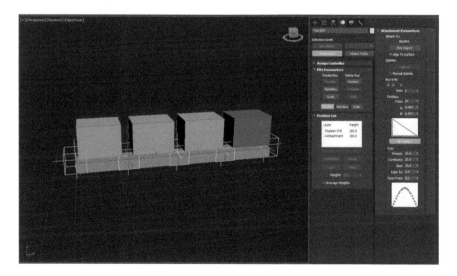

Figure 9.2

We have to use the *Set Position* option on the *Attachment Constraint* to place the *Point Helpers* correctly. From there, we use a *Position and Lookat Constraint* to keep the carriages attached and aligned properly.

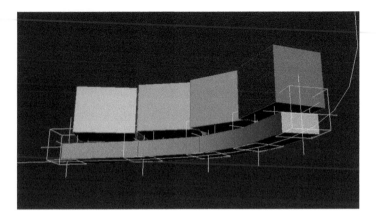

Figure 9.3

The finished setup allows us to connect a full rig to it easily. This means that we can work mostly on primitive objects to keep things simple, and then layer the complexities of the actual asset on top of it.

That pretty much covers this whole setup. You should be able to use the *Percentage* parameter to drive the setup and the attached train forward on the tracks. Now we can go ahead and start adjusting the track via the *path* that we have, and everything should update quickly and easily. Add the automatically rotating wheels, and you have a great train setup that sticks to the tracks perfectly (Figure 9.3).

9.2 Hydraulic Pistons

We covered the movement of pistons during the rigging of the steampunk locomotive in quite a bit of depth, and we even went into the mathematics to make sure that these pistons behave as expected at all times. What we missed out on were hydraulic pistons, like the kind that you find on diggers or other construction vehicles. This was a deliberate choice for the *NORAH* asset because rigging hydraulic pistons is not particularly difficult—at least it's not even close to the complexity of the pistons found on the train rig.

To rig a hydraulic piston, we need to use only a few *Lookat Constraints* with some *Point Helpers*, and everything works out great. It's important to remember that, unlike the real world, where these hydraulic pistons will actually create the movement for something, in the 3D-world, they simply move passively from other objects around them. So what we're doing here is to give the appearance that hydraulics is actually being used to move other objects.

Each hydraulic piston has two sections, upper and lower—I'm sure that they have some technical names, but for now "upper" and "lower" will do just fine. These two sections are then connected to their own *Point Helpers*. All we have to do for this rig is to use a *Lookat Constraint* on the bottom section that aims at the

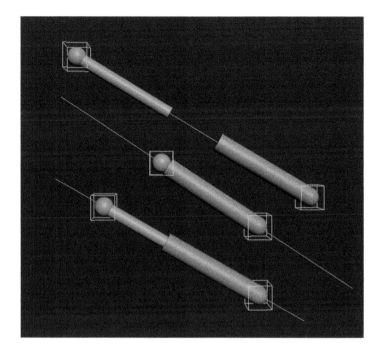

Figure 9.4

Setting up the hydraulic piston requires just the geometry, *Point Helpers*, and *Lookat Constraints* in order to create great-looking and technically accurate results.

upper *Point Helper.* Then we add another *Lookat Constraint* for the upper section, which points at the lower *Point Helper*...and that's really all there is to it. With this setup in place, we can use the *Point Helpers* to control the hydraulic piston, and it should behave exactly as we expect it to (Figure 9.4).

9.3 Animating Pivot Points

We covered pivots and movable pivots before we started rigging our *NORAH* asset, but we didn't actually create a pivot that we could move and animate. We should correct that right now!

You already know that the *pivot point* of an object is where we manipulate its *transforms*—the location where we can change the *Move, Rotate,* and *Scale* transforms, along with any other *deformers* that are attached to it. It may go without saying, but, there are times when it would be beneficial to be able to change the *pivot point* of an object. For instance, taking hold of the *OBJ_norahTrain1_layout_CTRL* allows us to move and rotate the train from a relatively intuitive spot. However, what happens if we need to pivot from another place, right now, in a situation where that's just not possible without the very real chance that we're going to break something else? Sure, we could add a *Point Helper* at that location and parent the controller to it, and then we could move and rotate that *Point Helper* from this new pivot location—but this sucks. No, really, it does. It's not only troublesome, but it totally changes the hierarchy of the rig—not a good thing.

Luckily, there is another way, and it's really easy to implement: You just have to know where to look, how to add it, and how to use it. Take hold of any old object in a new scene, and we'll add this to something where we don't care if it breaks or not. I mean, it shouldn't break at all, but you never know in the crazy world of Autodesk 3ds Max!

Now, head on over to the *Motion Tab* and under the *Assign Controller* rollout, select *Transform: Position/Rotation/Scale*. Click the *Assign Controller* button and choose the *CATHDPivotTrans* option in the newly opened window. With that controller highlighted, click the *OK* button. With the *CATHDPivotTrans* now active, nothing has happened just yet. We can still transform the controller as expected, from the original *Pivot Point* (Figure 9.5).

To allow us to edit the *Pivot Point*, click the *Sub-Object* button under the *Selection Level* area in the *Motion Tab*. This should enable the *PivotControls*, giving us direct access and the ability to manipulate and change the *Pivot Point* for each object. So, use the *Move* tool to edit the position of the *Pivot Point* for the controller. Disable the *Sub-Object* button, and now try rotating the selected object. At this point, you should be rotating from a whole new *Pivot Point* location—cool, huh?! Oh, and this can totally be animated. Bonus!!!

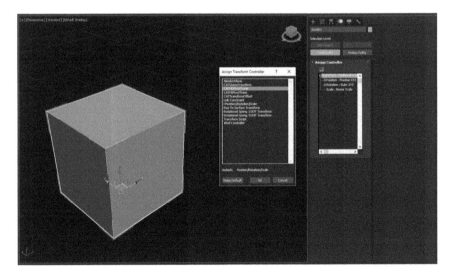

Figure 9.5

Adding an *animatable pivot* in 3ds Max is really easy—you just have to know where to put it and how to use it.

Adding an Animatable Pivot Point

Being able to animate the pivot point of an object can be an extremely rewarding (and often sought-after) feature that we can add to our rigs. This is useful for both organic and nonorganic rigs, and as it is very simple to apply in 3ds Max, it's worthwhile to add this feature where you think it will be necessary.

```
[SELECT OBJECT] > MOTION TAB > ASSIGN CATHDPIVOTTRANS > [SUB-
OBJECT MODE FROM THE MOTION TAB TO EDIT PIVOT]
```

Adding an animatable pivot point to controllers in your rigs is a great idea if you think that the additional control will be needed, or if it is a request or need for the production that you are working on. I've decided not to add these to the *NORAH* rig directly, as they are not really needed for this book. However, you can see that it would take very little time to add them yourself if you want. What's so great about this easy setup is the fact that you can add animatable pivots to rigs that you're already been working on, with no real fear of things breaking. Of course, there are a number of other ways to add pivot points that can be animated, but this is by far the easiest and one of the most robust ways I've used in 3ds Max.

9.4 Soft Tire Rigging

The wheels of a steampunk locomotive, or any train that I've heard of, are made completely of metal. You won't find tires on them anywhere. When I was first thinking about the steampunk train, I was contemplating having metal wheels run on the train tracks as they do now, but also having some huge, tractor-sized wheels that aren't on the tracks but are also helping to push it along. Far out! (Yeah, I attempted to use "cool" words there—forgive me.)

Anyway, that idea was quickly thrown in the trash, but air-filled rubber tires are a feature found on many vehicles and lots of construction machinery, among others.

To create a soft and squishy tire we need to use an *FFD(box)* element for this setup, but we won't be using the *FFD Modifier*. Instead, we'll be creating an *FFD(box)* object and attaching it to our geometry via the *Bind to Space Warp* option—I know, something different, yay!

OK—so as with everything in this chapter, I'm going to create some primitive geometry to illustrate a wheel. This is simply going to be two *Cylinders:* one larger to show the tire, and the other smaller to show the metal section of the wheel (the nondeformable part).

With the geometry in place, we can jump to the *Create Tab*, head over to the *Space Warps* button, go into *Geometric/Deformable,* and grab the *FFD(Box)* item. At this point, we can click-and-drag this out in the viewport, and in the *Modify*

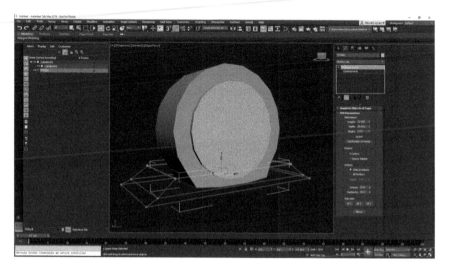

Figure 9.6

Soft tires are added easily by using the *FFD(Box)* object. Not to be confused with using *FFD Modifiers*, this method uses the *Bind to Space Warp* button to link *FFDs* to objects that we want to affect in our scene.

Tab, we can change the *Dimensions and Set Number of Points* as we need. I'm just putting this around the bottom section of the tire and changing the number of points to $2 \times 2 \times 4$ (Figure 9.6).

With the geometry and *FFD* in place, we can assign it to the geometry that we want to be affected by using the *Bind to Space Warps* button in a similar manner as we use the *Select and Link* tool. All that is left to do is grab the *FFD*, drop into its *Control Points* in *sub-object mode,* and edit the volume of the *FFD*. As you do this, you will notice that the geometry that we connected to it is automatically updated, but any geometry we didn't connect is not affected at all. Awesome, squishy-squashy tires are now ours!

Soft-Tire Setups

Setting up soft tires is a fun task that just requires an *FFD* object linked to the affected geometry via the *Bind to Space Warp* button. This method of geometry deformation is not limited to putting squishy tires on rigs—in fact, it has a number of uses, due to its ability to deform geometry as it passes through the affected area of the *FFD*.

```
CREATE TAB > SPACE WARPS > GEOMETRIC/DEFORMABLE > FFD(BOX)
```

9.5 Memory Refresh

See Table 9.1.

Table 9.1 **Memory Refresh: Animation and Automation Rig**

ADDING AN ANIMATABLE PIVOT POINT

```
[SELECT OBJECT] > MOTION TAB > ASSIGN CATHDPIVOTTRANS > [SUB-OBJECT
 MODE FROM THE MOTION TAB TO EDIT PIVOT]
```

SOFT TIRE SETUPS

```
CREATE TAB > SPACE WARPS > GEOMETRIC/DEFORMABLE > FFD(BOX)
```

9.6 Summary

In this chapter, we looked into four additional rigs and setups that we could use to enhance not only our *NORAH* asset, but also other mechanical creations in 3D. Two of the four techniques use the exact same tools that we've been using throughout this book, so they should be simple enough to implement by now— even though we are using them differently. The train tracks required us to use *World Space Modifiers (WSMs)* once again, but we attached *Point Helpers* using the *Attachment Constraint,* which is used a lot less often than the *Position constraint,* the *Link constraint,* and other tools. However, the hydraulic pistons involved a simple setup of some *Point Helpers* and *Lookat Constraints,* making them quick, fast, easy, and reliable to use on other mechanical geometries.

The other two projects rely on new ideas for us. For instance, the animatable pivot uses the built-in *CAT* animation system, which has the ability to include animatable pivots for free. So we simply grab that tool and use it in our own custom rigs instead—sneaky! We also looked at using *FFD* objects to deform geometry in our scene. Now, we have only scratched the surface of using this object, but what we have done here was to create an *FFD* object, rather than to use it as a *modifier,* which is, in my experience, the more common way to use this deformer.

Obviously, I applied these methods to primitive geometry rather than jumping back into the *NORAH* rig that we've been creating for the majority of this book. This is to illustrate the points here more easily, but also to make sure that the main chapters on rigging don't get confused with this chapter on additional techniques. I'm hopeful that you can see how (relatively) simple it will be to apply these new methods to the currently existing *NORAH* rig, as well as how, by using primitive objects, we can link up the real-life geometry to the primitive geometries we have created.

10

Conclusion

Whoa! Can you believe that we're at the end of our journey? We've successfully completed a steampunk locomotive rig, which we have come to call *NORAH*. During that time, this process has taken us through a basic introduction to everything, the analysis of the model, the chance to prepare for rigging, an overview of common rigging techniques, and an exploration of the various stages of the rigging process—the *Base Rig*, the *Animation and Automation Rig* (parts 1 and 2), and finally, the *Deformation Rig*.

To get here, we have looked at a vast array of tricks, tips, techniques, and methods used to deliver rigging solutions for mechanical objects. These complex and technical rigs were all created using the Autodesk 3ds Max software, but they could be translated into and re-created in any other professional three-dimensional (3D) software out there.

We then visited some additional methods for rigging mechanical geometry with things like train tracks, hydraulic pistons, fancy pivot points, and even the ability to squash tires or other geometry in our scene. Some of these techniques could even be applied to enhance the *NORAH* rig if we're feeling adventurous.

That's a lot of stuff for our brains to soak up as we've passed through this book. So where do we go from here?

10.1 Resources and Included Files

Available from DigitalRigging.com are the resources for this book. These files include all the textures for the *NORAH* asset, along with the following 3ds Max files:

- 00-OBJ_norah_START.max
- 01-OBJ_norah_GEO.max
- 02-OBJ_norah_BASE.max
- 03-OBJ_norah_RIG.max
- 04-OBJ_norah_COMPLETE.max

These files have been numbered so that you can see the start and end points for this rig, as well as some of the progress that has been made, as the rigging was a work in progress (WIP). If you would like to follow along in logical order with the chapters, simply open *00-OBJ_norah_START.max* and work from there. Or, if you would prefer to just check out the finished rig, take a look at *04-OBJ_norah_COMPLETE.max*, as this is the exact same file that was used for the rendering found on the front cover.

10.2 *NORAH*: The Front Cover

As already mentioned, the finished art for the front cover of this book, shown in Figure 10.1, was created using the *04-OBJ_norah_COMPLETE.max,* and the

Figure 10.1

The final rendering of the front cover features the completed *NORAH* rig, its controllers, train tracks, and even some smoke and dust.

same file was used for the same train tracks setup in Chapter 9, "More Mechanical Rigging." Smoke, steam, and dust were added using the built-in *Particle Flow* system in 3ds Max, and the image was completed using the *Arnold* renderer, which is also included in newer versions of the software.

I always make every attempt to do all the work in these books using only a default version of 3ds Max—that means no plug-ins, no tricks, and nothing fancy like custom-scripted tools. This means that you should be able to follow along perfectly without having to rely on any additional software or applications. This isn't always easy because some amazing plug-ins and tools are available to make our lives easier. However…

One additional software program that was needed for the texture work on the *NORAH* asset, the front cover, and some of the images found in this book was Adobe Photoshop. Photoshop helped me compile the cover image, as I rendered multiple layers both to speed up rendering time and achieve the effects I needed and wanted. I'm sure that you either have this software already, have used it, or at least have heard of it, as it is an industry standard. At this time, I'm using PhotoshopCC, which is the latest version that comes with a subscription to this software. Unfortunately, as seems to be a common approach these days (I might be showing my age here), Photoshop, just like 3ds Max for that matter, requires a month-by-month payment in order to have the latest version.

10.3 Memory Refresh Is Missing!

There is nothing in this chapter that needs a "memory refresh" of any kind, but I hope that these sections throughout this book have been helpful to you. The "Memory Refresh" sections have been designed to be places where you can go for quick and easy guidance into the many techniques used throughout the rigging of the *NORAH* asset, as well as the rigs that we created as examples for various rigging methods. These sections are by no means a comprehensive guide, but simply a quick listing of where various tools are found in 3ds Max, and what techniques or methods have been used during each chapter. Maybe the next time that you're up against a challenging rig of some kind, you will remember to look to these "memory refresh" areas to find that spark of inspiration to get you through a difficult rigging problem.

10.4 What Next?

The most logical step in the process for complete rigging domination (not an actual thing) is to incorporate all the extra features that we looked at in Chapters 8 and 9 into the *NORAH* rig. This would enhance the steampunk locomotive even further and make it the best possible rig it can be. From there, the choice is entirely up to you.

You could move on to your own mechanical model, or one for a production that you are working on, and implement all the techniques we have covered during the pages of this book. Alternatively, you could take this newly gained knowledge and try it in an alternative 3D software. If you're familiar with another application already, this shouldn't be too difficult, but if you're new to other 3D software, it's going to be another big challenge.

If you have enjoyed this book and wish to increase your knowledge of rigging in 3ds Max, there are another two books out there that I have written:

- *Digital Creature Rigging: The Art and Science of CG Creature Setup in 3ds Max* (Jones, S. [2012], USA, Focal Press)
- *Digital Creature Rigging: Wings, Tails, and Tentacles* (Jones, S. [2019], USA, Focal Press)

Both offer a unique look at how to create production-ready rigs for creatures, and they use the same methodologies found in this book, including the 3 Stage Asset Build (3SAB) approach, among others. Oh, and you'll find more great assets from Chris and myself in there too. Woop!

10.5 A Quick Note

While all the rigs featured in this book are available to you, if you do decide to use one of these rigs or models for your own work, both Chris and myself would love it if you could credit us in some way. We'd also really like to see what you come up with, so feel free to send us a message and link us up with your work—we're pretty easy to find online, with links to our social media accounts and websites in the "About the Author" section at the start of this book, and online at DigitalRigging.com.

Of course, you don't have to do this, but, if we have helped you in any way, we are genuinely interested in the work that you create using our assets and techniques. We've been flattered by your responses when you've reached out to us in the past, and we really try our very best to give you some great content and information.

Thank you in advance.

10.6 Goodbye and Good Luck

This is really the end for our journey together at this point. We have succeeded in our goals, and the road ahead is a blank page in a new book somewhere…or at least a freshly opened scene in the 3D world!

I once again need to give a big shout-out to my friend, the talented Chris Rocks, for all of his hard work and dedicated to the 3D model and textures that became the most amazing asset and highlight for this book. It also became far more challenging than either of us anticipated, even with all of our planning.

Thank you so much for taking this journey into *Mechanical Creations in 3D* with me. Together, we've taken "A Practical Look into Complex and Technical

Setups for Animation & VFX." I hope that what I've shared with you has helped increase or solidify your rigging knowledge, and that this book becomes a trusty guide for you to refer to in your future rigging challenges.

It means a great deal to me that you decided to choose this book as your learning material. If you see Chris or me out there in your real-world adventures be sure to say hello—it's always great to hear whether our hard work has helped you with your development into the crazy world of computer graphics and entertainment.

Goodbye, and the very best of luck on your journey ahead...

Index

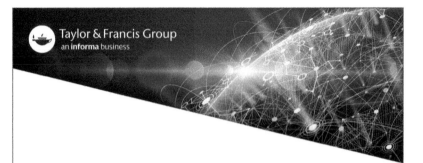

Taylor & Francis eBooks

www.taylorfrancis.com

A single destination for eBooks from Taylor & Francis
with increased functionality and an improved user
experience to meet the needs of our customers.

90,000+ eBooks of award-winning academic content in
Humanities, Social Science, Science, Technology, Engineering,
and Medical written by a global network of editors and authors.

TAYLOR & FRANCIS EBOOKS OFFERS:

A streamlined
experience for
our library
customers

A single point
of discovery
for all of our
eBook content

Improved
search and
discovery of
content at both
book and
chapter level

REQUEST A FREE TRIAL
support@taylorfrancis.com

Milton Keynes UK
Ingram Content Group UK Ltd.
UKHW021527161024
449569UK00059B/4

9 781138 560505